# "Did You Say Something, Susan?"

# *"Did You Say Something, Susan?"*

## How Any Woman Can Gain Confidence With Assertive Communication

### Paulette Dale, Ph.D.

A BIRCH LANE PRESS BOOK
Published by Carol Publishing Group

A Birch Lane Press Book
Published by Carol Publishing Group
Birch Lane Press is a registered trademark of Carol Communications, Inc.

Editorial, sales and distribution, rights and permissions inquiries should be
addressed to Carol Publishing Group, 120 Enterprise Avenue, Secaucus, N.J.
07094.

In Canada: Canadian Manda Group, One Atlantic Avenue, Suite 105, Toronto,
Ontario, M6K 3E7

Carol Publishing Group books may be purchased in bulk at special discounts
for sales promotion, fund-raising, or educational purposes. Special editions can
be created to specifications. For details, contact Special Sales Department,
Carol Publishing Group, 120 Enterprise Avenue, Secaucus, N.J. 07094.

Manufactured in the United States of America
10  9  8  7  6  5  4  3  2  1

Library of Congress Cataloging-in-Publication Data

Dale, Paulette.
    "Did you say something, Susan?" : how any woman can gain confidence
with assertive communication / Paulette Wainless Dale.
        p.   cm.
    "A Birch Lane Press book."
    Includes bibliographical references (p.  ).
    ISBN 1–55972–482–X (hardcover)
    1. Assertiveness in women.    2. Assertiveness training.
3. Interpersonal communication.    4. Self-confidence.   I. Title.
HQ1206.D325   1998
158.2′082—dc21                                      98–25277
                                                        CIP

# Contents

To my parents, Ephraim and Anne Wainless, and to my brother, Ira Wainless, for providing me with the kind of loving, supportive environment that has enabled me to live my life with a positive self-image, the strength of my convictions, and the courage to express them.

# *Preface*

*If all my talents and powers were taken from me by some inscrutable Providence, and I had my choice of keeping but one, I would choose to keep the Power of Communication, for through it, I would quickly recover all the rest.*

—DANIEL WEBSTER

Who is Susan, you may be wondering? You're Susan. I'm Susan. Susan is every woman who has ever kicked herself for being reluctant or too timid to speak up for herself.

Lack of confidence, insecurity, and the private dread that they are inferior to others plague millions of women regardless of educational background or socioeconomic level. For many of you, it may be particularly difficult to communicate forcefully and confidently. However, the ability to do so affects how successful you are in personal and professional relationships. The ability to communicate directly and assertively also affects how often your opinions are listened to, how seriously you are taken, and how much respect others have for you.

I wrote this book to show you how to experience the exhilaration and emotional freedom of saying what you want to say in any given situation. *"Did You Say Something, Susan?"* presents practical but powerful techniques to motivate and inspire you to become an assertive communicator. By following the advice, you will become empowered to take responsibility for your own emotional well-being.

After years of observing various women in my life—friends, colleagues, relatives, students—I realized that the vast majority are not taken as seriously as they would like to be and don't know what to do about it.

These women are timid about expressing their innermost thoughts for fear of sounding foolish. They hesitate to express displeasure with deficient services or to return defective products. They are reluctant to voice their opinions in a group or ask questions without first apologizing for being a bother. They are afraid to defend themselves verbally or speak up when they are treated poorly or wronged in some way. They prefer, instead, to depend on the males in their lives to do the talking on their behalf. They are frequently ready to accept blame and criticism without verbal protest in the interest of "keeping the peace" and not triggering a conflict.

However, many women are weary of kicking themselves for what they "should have said" and of feeling so helpless in the face of verbal abuse. Since I am a professional in the area of effective communication, they frequently ask me for guidance.

These delightful multitalented women include students, teachers, performers, engineers, attorneys, accountants, college professors, housewives, and mothers. Many of them grew up with all the material advantages, yet they still have debilitating feelings of inadequacy, insecurity, and inferiority. Being blessed with intelligence, wit, beauty, and talent does not guarantee that a woman also possesses a positive self-image.

My experience with hundreds of individuals has taught me that effective assertive communication is the quickest, most direct route to developing lifelong feelings of confidence, self-respect, and the admiration of others. I wrote *"Did You Say Something, Susan?"* with the hope that it would inspire as many women as possible to develop a stronger sense of self: self-worth, self-esteem, self-respect, self-concept through assertive communication.

Life should be a joy for these women, whom I care so much about. Yet they have not regularly experienced the exhilaration and

~~uuniuu ui uiiuviuiiiil Liuuuli.iiii iiiil i iiiii.ii, liimi iimliulii iiiij iiiiiiliiii~~
it is they might want to say in any given situation.

Do these women sound like anyone you know? Perhaps you recognize yourself. If so, you should feel really good that you are ready to do something about it. By following the ten-step program presented in *"Did You Say Something, Susan?"* you will:

- Learn to say what you really feel.
- Learn to say no and mean it.
- Speak up for your rights.
- Get what you need on your terms.
- Become confident and articulate.
- Gain the respect and admiration of others.

This book offers you a variety of strategies. It will serve as your advisor and counselor. You will be able to put the advice offered into immediate practice. Follow the steps; the advice is sound, and the program really works. As the famous Nike slogan says, "Just Do It!" You will gain a newfound confidence and sense of self-respect.

Direct, assertive communication is the key to getting the results you want when dealing with people. Having the confidence to express what you feel and think will make life a lot more fun. So, exercise your verbal skills and become an assertive communicator. Gain courage and confidence. Your personal advisor—*"Did You Say Something, Susan?"* will guide you.

Good luck, and let's begin!

# Introduction:
# A Commitment to Change

*You gain strength, courage and confidence by every experience in which you really stop to look fear in the face. You must do the thing you think you cannot do.*

—ELEANOR ROOSEVELT

My first summer job in the "real world" was as a showroom model at 1407 Broadway in New York City's garment district. I was seventeen years old. I had not yet learned that miserable souls were everywhere lurking in the shadows seeking an opportunity to pounce and demean anyone whose guard was down. The showroom manager requested that I model a newly designed outfit to compare it with several styles already displayed on mannequins in the corner of the room. Pointing to the mannequins, he ordered me, "Go stand over there with the other dummies." Too intimidated to protest this insult, I did as I was told.

Even as I left work that day, I couldn't shake off the feeling of humiliation. Relating the episode to my family during dinner, I was expecting innocuous platitudes like, "Just forget it. Don't let what happened bother you." Instead, my father asked how I responded. I explained I had said nothing. He smashed his fist on the table and shouted, "Since when have you become mute? How dare you allow yourself to be spoken to that way! You are inferior to no one and *don't ever forget it!*" Needless to say, I never have. Twenty-nine years later, my outraged father's remark at the dinner table — "Since when have you become mute?"—served as the catalyst for this book.

I had my parents' help in making the commitment to believe in my self-worth. I credit them for providing me with the kind of loving, supportive environment that has enabled me to live my life with a positive self-image, the strength of my convictions, and the courage to express them. They taught me to speak up and say what I feel. I could not have done it by myself. You don't have to do it by yourself, either. Come with me and allow this book to serve as your coach and counselor as my father served as mine.

Women tend to use their lack of confidence as an excuse to avoid communicating assertively. When I encouraged my friend Paige to stand up to a neighbor who had been taking advantage of her for years, she became defensive. "That's easy for you to say, Paulette. If I had your personality, I'd be able to speak up, too. I just don't have the confidence to do it."

I wasn't always verbally fit. I didn't always have the courage and confidence to speak up. But I did it anyway. It's the old dilemma, "Which comes first, the chicken or the egg?" Or, in this case, which comes first: speaking up or feeling confident?

In *How to Stubbornly Refuse to Make Yourself Miserable About Anything,* psychologist Dr. Albert Ellis writes, "Our feelings arise from complex thoughts and philosophies. As Epictetus and Marcus Aurelius, ancient philosophers, pointed out, we humans mainly feel the way we think."

In other words, you don't need to feel a certain way in order to speak a certain way. Don't wait to feel self-confidence before you are willing to speak up. Begin your program of verbal fitness now. The confidence will come later! As William James said, "If you want a quality, act as if you already had it. Try the 'as if' technique." Actress Goldie Hawn was quoted in the September 1996 issue of *Ladies' Home Journal,* "Challenge yourself, face your fears. Whatever it is, you think, I'm afraid to say it, and suddenly when you say it, the fear goes away." Jiminy Cricket in *Pinocchio* had the right idea also. Whenever he felt afraid, he whistled a happy tune so that no one would suspect he was afraid. And by whistling his tune long enough, he suddenly wasn't afraid anymore. So, *act as if* … it really works!

Take some time to think about the problems you have expressing your thoughts and feelings. The following twenty questions were inspired by the Assertiveness Inventory in *Your Perfect Right* by Robert Alberti and Michael Emmons. Use them as a guide to analyze your ability to express your feelings in general.

1. Do you hesitate to speak up when treated unfairly?
2. Are you reluctant to ask a person to pay back money owed to you?
3. Do you hesitate to remind someone to return a possession borrowed from you?
4. Do you remain silent if someone cuts in front of you in line?
5. Would you avoid telling a neighbor you are bothered by his barking dog?
6. Would you tell someone it's okay to smoke in your presence even if the smoke bothers you?
7. Do you frequently say yes when you want to say no to inconvenient requests?
8. Are you reluctant to complain about rude service?
9. Do you generally hesitate to stand up for your rights?
10. Do you remain silent when someone insults you or puts you down?
11. Do you have difficulty making your needs or preferences clear to others?
12. Do you avoid expressing your opinions in a group when you know others are likely to disagree with you?
13. Are you reluctant to complain about improperly served or prepared food in a restaurant?
14. When a person does something to offend you, do you avoid mentioning it?
15. Would you change your seat at a movie rather than ask a noisy individual to speak softly?
16. Would you shut your window rather than tell a neighbor's children their loud music is disturbing?
17. Do you apologize before asking questions in class or at meetings?

18. ~~Do you have friends with questions for you in class or at~~
    meetings?
19. Do you preface comments with disclaimers such as "I may
    be wrong" or "I may have misunderstood but…?"
20. Do you generally bite your tongue to keep peace or avoid a
    conflict?

One yes response to any of the above questions is one yes too
many! Why should you hesitate to express yourself with anyone in
any situation? Being able to speak up is one of your greatest
personal freedoms. It allows you to fully participate in all life has to
offer.

It's important to understand that assertiveness depends upon
the situation and the individual involved. Most people are what
psychologists call split assertives. In other words, no one is
assertive all the time or with all people. Even extremely confident
women find themselves reluctant to speak up with certain
individuals. The most verbally adept among us often becomes
tongue-tied in particular situations.

For example, my friend Candy is a poised, sassy trial lawyer. She
will challenge any judge or attorney in court but won't send back
the wrong order in a restaurant or say what she thinks in personal
situations for fear of being rejected. Angela, on the other hand, is
timid about communicating her ideas at work but quite assertive
when communicating with friends or family. Lisa, who usually
stands up to everyone and everything, couldn't fire her house-
keeper and waited until she quit on her own. There are some
women who can express their opinions to other women but never
to men and vice versa. What is a difficult situation for one person is
a piece of cake for another. As you can see, it's perfectly natural to
feel confident in some circumstances and insecure in others.

### Forget What You Learned As a Child

Many girls grow up hearing variations on the "children should be
seen but not heard" theme. Many of us have been encouraged to

keep our opinions and ideas to ourselves. Most of us grew up hearing, "It's not ladylike to talk back," "Be quiet and don't make waves," "Think it but don't say it," or "If you don't have anything nice to say, don't say anything at all."

This type of advice may have produced your belief that your thoughts and feelings should not be expressed. Wrong! You were born to talk and express yourself. Without realizing it, you've been trained to be seen but not heard. Well, guess what? You can change this behavior that you were trained to accept. You no longer have to live your life inhibited by the "think it but don't say it" philosophy. Just as you learned to be passive, you can learn to become assertive. Assertive communication is a skill, as is speaking a foreign language, playing the piano, or knowing how to sew. Just as these skills are learned and perfected, so is the ability to communicate with confidence.

### It's Never Too Late

You might be thinking, "It's too late for me," "I can never think of anything to say," "I get upset at the thought of speaking up," or "I've always been like that, I can't change now."

These are the messages so ingrained in your mind. They are not true! You absolutely can change if you really want to. No one is born passive, submissive, or indirect. These communication styles are the result of past experiences and learning. It's possible to change these unrewarding ways of communicating. Thousands of people have successfully done it. You can, too!

After reading a draft of *"Did You Say Something, Susan?"* my middle-aged secretary, Elaine, rushed into the office. "I finally did it!" she cried, elatedly. "You finally did what?" I asked, perplexed. "I finally summoned up enough courage to tell Nina, the dean's assistant, to stop pointing her index finger at me like a weapon when she talks. She's been doing it for years. I should have told her a long time ago." Elaine's elation was contagious. Punching the air with my fist, I whispered an emphatic Yes!

Martha, a great-grandmother in her seventies, had always been shy and submissive. She always worried that people might think

~~she was *firstly* if she disagreed with anyone or complained about~~ anything. Arriving early for a doctor's appointment, Martha was kept waiting for over an hour. The physician, anxious to make up for lost time, rushed through his appointment with her. He abruptly said, "Everything is fine, Martha. Just keep taking your medicine as always." Martha timidly attempted to ask a question about a side effect caused by the medication. The doctor abruptly cut her off, "I don't have time to talk. I have lots of patients waiting." Martha decided right then and there, *It's now or never. I'm sick and tired of being treated like a nobody, and I'm not going to take it anymore.* She asserted herself by saying, "Well, Dr. Miles, make time! I waited an hour to see you. Now it's my turn. I have a concern I'd like to discuss. Please don't dismiss me so rapidly." Dr. Miles sheepishly apologized and addressed Martha's concerns. Martha reported she never felt better. She laughed, "Speaking up turned out to be the best medicine of all!"

As you can see, whether you are seventeen or seventy-seven, it's never too late. You must believe you are capable of changing your communication style and that you are truly worthy of being listened to and treated with respect.

## Change Comes Gradually

Successfully changing the way you communicate does take effort. Becoming verbally fit is no different than becoming physically fit. It takes commitment, and it takes exercise.

Please don't feel discouraged or overwhelmed by this prospect of transformation. You don't need to change instantly or completely. Your goal is improvement. Improving your ability to communicate assertively is best done gradually. It's not necessary to read this book from cover to cover all at once. In fact, it's not even necessary to read each chapter in its entirety in one sitting. It may be better to read one or two points about each step in the program and then to think carefully about them before continuing.

Take the time to complete the various exercises throughout the book. They will help you better understand and become comfortable with the various techniques. Remember, in order to become verbally fit, you need to *exercise.* The various activities will help you practice the techniques necessary to express yourself easily and confidently.

*"Did You Say Something, Susan?"* presents a ten-step program to help you develop respect and self-confidence with assertive communication. However, it is not necessary to learn the techniques all at once. Nor is it necessary to follow them in a set sequence. The program is designed to be flexible. Where you begin will depend largely upon your responses to the self-assessment on pages xvii through xix. The book is also designed to be used as a handy reference. Refer to it often. Choose the advice that will help you handle a situation as it arises. For example, if you need immediate advice about how to respond to an insult or put-down, go right to chapter 8: "Don't Put Up With Put-Downs." If you need some moral support to firmly say "no" to an unreasonable request made by a friend or family member, turn directly to chapter 4: "Just Say 'No'."

A variety of exercises are here to help you practice. Select the ones you are most comfortable trying and which suit your personality. Don't feel overwhelmed. Change comes little by little. It's not necessary to take large leaps to communicate more assertively—unless you really want to. Smaller, gradual steps will work just fine. Take situations as they pop up in your life. *"Did You Say Something, Susan?"* will help you work through them one at a time.

### You Are Not Alone

As you progress and experiment with using assertive speech and body language, responding to put-downs, being more direct, saying a firm "No," or "I need time to think it over," or "That's not acceptable," think of me as your coach and counselor. Pretend I'm standing beside you and offering you moral support when you find yourself in a situation where you are reluctant to say what you really want to say. Visualize me encouraging you to speak up for yourself. Hear me remind you, "Say what you really feel, and say it now!"

E-mail me (pwodulu@aol.com) with your experiences. I want to share your successes, triumphs, and elation. Remember, all is not lost if you suffer a temporary lapse and slip back into old habit patterns. That's perfectly normal and to be expected. After all, change is difficult but it is not impossible. Never become frustrated or angry with yourself for your lack of assertion in a particular situation. You will have another opportunity to "rise to the occasion."

As you learn and practice the responses you are taught in *"Did You Say Something, Susan?"* you will be rewarded with empowering and exhilarating feelings of self-esteem. A strong self-concept is vital if you hope to successfully face the trials and tribulations that arise in daily life. Self-respect is the key to the way you treat yourself and are treated by others. You will gain the confidence you want and deserve by making the commitment to exercise assertive communication.

## Assess Yourself

The following self-assessment test will help you to more specifically analyze your ability to communicate assertively in a variety of situations. Once you analyze the results, you'll be directed to the sections of the book that will benefit you the most. Consider the following statements and circle the number that describes you the best. *1* means Usually; *2* means Often; *3* means Sometimes; and *4* means Never.

1. Others find it easy to take advantage of me.            1 2 3 4
2. There are a few people who make jokes at my            1 2 3 4
   expense or put me down repeatedly.
3. I hesitate to speak up for fear others might            1 2 3 4
   consider me aggressive rather than assertive.
4. Others say I misunderstand what they tell me.            1 2 3 4
5. I sound like I'm asking a question when I'm            1 2 3 4
   making a statement.
6. I tend to look down at the floor or fold my arms            1 2 3 4
   across my chest when speaking to others.

7.  I tend to preface my comments with disclaimers    1 2 3 4
    such as "I may be wrong" or "This might be a
    stupid question but...."

8.  I tend to say too much and give too many details    1 2 3 4
    when I explain something.

9.  I tend to downplay compliments when I receive    1 2 3 4
    them.

10. I avoid expressing my displeasure for fear that    1 2 3 4
    others will tell me that I'm too sensitive or else
    criticize me in some other way.

11. I tend to bite my tongue to keep the peace.    1 2 3 4

12. Others make me feel guilty when I say no to    1 2 3 4
    their requests.

13. I feel the need to invent excuses when I say no.    1 2 3 4

14. I tend to provide numerous reasons rather than a    1 2 3 4
    brief justification when I say no.

15. I tend to say yes when I want to say no.    1 2 3 4

16. I feel guilty when I say no.    1 2 3 4

17. I make promises I later regret.    1 2 3 4

18. I allow myself to be pressured into making snap    1 2 3 4
    decisions.

19. I tend to respond impetuously rather than    1 2 3 4
    carefully choosing my words.

20. I feel compelled to follow through with decisions    1 2 3 4
    I've made even when I don't feel good about
    them.

21. I accept what I'm offered even when it's not what    1 2 3 4
    I wanted or expected.

22. I tend to remain silent when treated unfairly.    1 2 3 4

23. I allow myself to be inconvenienced in order to    1 2 3 4
    avoid conflicts.

24. I tend to beat around the bush rather than    1 2 3 4
    express my feelings directly.

25. I ask friends or family members to speak for me    1 2 3 4
    when I'm reluctant to speak up for myself.

26. I feel that prefacing my own opinions with "My    1 2 3 4
    *husband [boyfriend, father]* says...", or "My *boss*
    says...," gives my words more credibility.
27. I tend to kick myself for what I should have said.    1 2 3 4
28. I tend to respond defensively when unfairly    1 2 3 4
    criticized.
29. On the spur-of-the-moment, I can never think of    1 2 3 4
    clever come-backs to rude remarks.
30. I tend to suffer in silence when unfairly criticized    1 2 3 4
    or insulted.
31. I feel uncomfortable taking credit for my own    1 2 3 4
    accomplishments.
32. I'm more reluctant to speak up on the job than in    1 2 3 4
    other situation.
33. I'm reluctant to say no when my supervisor    1 2 3 4
    makes unfair or inconvenient requests.
34. I lose my courage at the last moment and don't    1 2 3 4
    say what I planned to say when faced with an
    awkward or threatening situation.
35. When I'm nervous about an upcoming event or    1 2 3 4
    situation, I have doubts about my ability to
    handle it as successfully as I'd like.

OK, now that you've completed the assessment, you're ready to analyze your responses. There are no numbers to add up! There's no good or bad score! The statements are designed to help you identify the areas for you to focus on in *"Did You Say Something, Susan?"* For example, if you responded Usually, Often, or even Sometimes, to statements 5, 6, 7, 8, or 9, the information in chapter 2 will really help you.

Use the following chart to determine which chapters will benefit you the most based on your responses to the self-assessment.

| Self-Assessment Statements | Relevant Chapter |
|---|---|
| 1-4 | 1. Be Unappealing to Users and Abusers |
| 5-9 | 2. Adopt Assertive Speech and Body Language |
| 10-12 | 3. Prepare for Confrontation |
| 13-16 | 4. Just Say "No" |
| 17-20 | 5. Buy Time Before Responding |
| 21-23 | 6. "That's Not Acceptable" |
| 24-26 | 7. Speak for Yourself |
| 27-30 | 8. Don't Put Up With Put-Downs |
| 31-33 | 9. Speak Up on the Job |
| 34-35 | 10. Go for It! |

Once you identify which assertive communication skills to practice, why not get started right away! I recommend beginning by perfecting those areas to which you responded *3* (Sometimes). Those will be the easiest for you to improve. Then, analyze the statements to which you responded *2* (Often), and work on the corresponding chapters. Once you're really confident in the areas to which you responded *2* and *3*, you'll be ready to tackle the chapters corresponding with the statements to which you responded *1* (Usually). These will challenge you the most. After you've worked on the various assertive communication skills, take the self-assessment again. I bet you'll be pleasantly surprised to find that you've circled more *3*'s and *4*'s than before. Keep practicing the skills taught here and you'll soon be communicating confidently and effectively in most situations!

# "Did You Say Something, Susan?"

# 1

# *Be Unappealing to Users and Abusers*

Eve, a talented and successful interior designer, put the following question to me over coffee one morning: "Am I putting out some signal that says to the world at large, 'Go ahead, kick me and humiliate me if you want to?'" "What ever are you talking about?" I inquired. Eve plaintively continued, "What is it about me that people think they can insult me, intimidate me, or ask me inappropriate questions whenever they feel like it? Why do they walk all over me but they don't walk all over you?" My answer was immediate. "Because you let them. People will treat you the way you teach them to treat you."

It was my conversation with Eve that led me to consider the problem of why some individuals are picked on more often than others. I assured Eve that she was not putting out signals inviting users and abusers to take advantage of her. She is in no way responsible for initially attracting them. However, her do-nothing, say-nothing reaction encourages them to keep returning. Her silence implies her consent. Some people are hungry for ego satisfaction, and they seek it anywhere and with anyone for as long as they're allowed to get away with it.

3

## Users and Abusers Love Easy Targets

On one occasion, Eve loaned her car to Doreen, who needed it for a quick errand. Doreen got around to returning the car two days later with an empty gas tank and no explanation. Although Eve was extremely hurt and annoyed, she accepted her car keys silently. She bit her tongue to keep the peace.

On another occasion, Doreen borrowed Eve's formal dress. She returned it, apologizing for several wine stains, but never offered to dry-clean the dress or pay to have it dry-cleaned. Fuming inside, Eve wordlessly accepted the garment.

In a professional situation, a corporate CEO hired Eve to redecorate his suite of offices. In meetings with the CEO's staff, Eve was the target of a series of dumb-blonde jokes. Not wanting to make waves, she suffered in silence until completing the job.

All in all, Eve was an easy target and was treated as such. By remaining silent, she allowed all these people to use and abuse her. Instead of being subjected to one dumb-blonde joke, she suffered a series of them. Eve needed to practice verbal fitness and speak up for herself.

The users and abusers are like mosquitoes buzzing around looking for exposed flesh to bite. If one bites and you do nothing, it will be back to bite again and again. If you have quick reflexes and flatten it with a clap between your palms, it can't return to bother you.

Unfortunately, there is no shortage of mosquitoes, nor is there a shortage of users and abusers waiting to impose their will on you, criticize you, take advantage of you, and make themselves feel superior by making you feel inferior. But you don't have to let them. It's your choice, not theirs. If you seem like an easy target, they will use you for target practice. By learning the assertive communication techniques presented in this book, you will develop your verbal reflexes. You will be able to respond swiftly and decisively. Just like the squashed mosquitoes, these freeloaders and verbal bullies won't be back.

Although you may feel that something in your demeanor or manner *attracts* these toxic types to you like a magnet, that is not

the ones. Think of yourself as a nice home in a nice neighborhood
with no security system. You have done nothing out of the ordinary
to call attention to yourself. You're not wearing a sign that
announces "Enter my home; steal from me." Nevertheless, thieves
will find you as they go from house to house trying to find an
unlocked door or window. When they find it, that's the house
they'll enter. They're looking for an easy score. They won't stop
until the owners start making entry more difficult. Only then, will
the burglars move on.

Don't wait until you are completely robbed of your confidence,
self-respect, and dignity before taking action. Become an assertive
communicator to deflect the users and abusers!

I'm sure you understand the analogy. You are in no way at fault
for the users or put-you-downers who initially approach you. Their
lives are probably so unsatisfying that they try to entertain
themselves by verbally abusing people who allow them to.
However, you do need to take responsibility if you give the
appearance of encouraging these opportunists' interest in you.
Lock your doors, communicate assertively, and these predators will
go elsewhere, seeking easier prey.

### Assertive Doesn't Mean Aggressive

Unfortunately, too many women have been brought up to be
submissive "pleasers." They get confused when they want to speak
for themselves. They believe they will be viewed as aggressive or
unpleasant if they speak up. Therefore, they mistakenly go to the
other extreme. In an effort to avoid coming across as aggressive,
they react in a submissive manner. Women who regularly use this
submissive or nonassertive communication style report feelings of
inferiority and low self-esteem. They often harbor anger and
resentment toward those who take advantage of them. There is a
huge difference between polite, assertive responses and the
extremes of submissive or aggressive ones.

A *submissive* reaction conveys the message "*I'm* not impor-
tant/*You're* important" and indicates you don't consider yourself
equal to others. It encourages users and abusers to repeatedly walk

all over you. Submissive people fear that expressing their true feelings might rock the boat. They don't get what they want because they won't stand up for themselves.

An *aggressive* response conveys the opposite message. "*I'm* all important/You're *nothing*" and implies that you consider your rights and wishes to have more value than those of others. It boldly indicates you expect your needs to be accommodated at others' expense. Aggressive communicators tend to verbally attack people as well as issues they dislike.

An *assertive* reply conveys the message "*I'm* important/You're important/We're *both* important" and shows you will value and protect your own rights without infringing on the rights of others. It shows respect for others while simultaneously maintaining your own self-respect. Assertive speaking is clear, direct and to the point. It expresses your wishes in a positive, self-confident way and increases your sense of personal worth.

Participants in my workshops are hesitant and resistant when I first encourage them to say "no" to unreasonable requests or let someone know when they are out of line. I'm met with doubtful glances and apprehensive comments: "I feel so guilty when I say no," "I don't want to cause any problems or hurt anyone," "I'd rather be insulted than insult someone else."

"But that's the beauty of assertive communication," I explain. "You don't have to offend anyone or feel guilty for protecting your own rights. You can speak up for yourself while showing respect for others' feelings."

In *Your Perfect Right,* psychologists Alberti and Emmons offer wonderful clarification between assertiveness and aggressiveness. They state, "Assertiveness is often confused with aggressiveness, so let's clear that up right now. Learning to be more assertive does not mean learning to push other folks around in order to get your way. It does mean standing up for yourself, expressing feelings directly and firmly, establishing equal relationships that take the needs of both people into account."

The following examples will further help you understand the differences between submissive, aggressive, and assertive communication.

A cigarette smoker asks if you object to his/her smoking in your car.

A submissive reply, even though you are allergic to or extremely bothered by the smoke, would be, "No problem, that's fine if you really want to." (This conveys the message, "I'm not important. I will inhibit my preference and defer to yours at my expense.")

An *aggressive* response would be, "Yes, I most certainly do object. You are very rude and inconsiderate to even consider subjecting me to secondhand smoke. I refuse to allow smoking in my car." (This conveys, "I'm more important than you." In addition to rejecting the request, it attacks the person as well.)

An *assertive* reaction might be, "Thank you for asking. I'd prefer you didn't. It really bothers me. Would you like me to pull over so you could smoke a cigarette outside? I'd be happy to stop whenever you like." (This response conveys, "We're both important." You directly and clearly asserted your needs while respecting those of your passenger. You recognized your friend's desire to smoke without sacrificing your preference that there be no smoking in your car. You've orchestrated a win-win situation through assertive communication.)

Here's another example. You're next in line at the drugstore pharmacy counter, waiting to pick up a prescription. A man taps you on the shoulder saying, "Excuse me, honey, I'm late for an important meeting. May I go ahead of you?" You, too, are in a rush, with a sick child to get home to.

A *submissive* reply would be, "Sure, okay." (This conveys the message, "You're more important than I am. Your time is more valuable than mine.")

An *aggressive* response would be, "Absolutely not. You're a pushy chauvinist. You wouldn't have asked that if I were a man. Go to the end of the line like everyone else." (This conveys, "You're nothing." You belligerently attack the person as well as deny the request.)

An *assertive* reaction might be, "No, I'm really in a hurry also. I understand your urgency, though. Why don't you ask someone else to let you in the line." (This response conveys, "You're important, but I'm important too." You stood up for yourself while respecting the other customer's right to request a favor. You meant no offense by denying the request; none was taken. Again, you orchestrated a win-win situation with assertive communication.)

Assertive communication, like any skill, takes practice. You might overdo it initially or continue to underdo it for a while. Practice with family and friends. Let them know what you're doing so they won't be abruptly surprised by the new you. It's similar to perfecting a new recipe—a trial-and-error process. At first, you may use too much of one ingredient and too little of another, but you persevere until you get it just right! It's like you have given your friends taste tests and then examined their expressions to see how they enjoyed your new dish. Their rave reviews or helpful hints will motivate you to keep up your efforts and search for new ways to improve a little each time.

Summon up the courage to try out your new repertoire of retorts and responses on people with whom you interact. Don't worry or be discouraged if you trip up at first. Observe and assess their reactions and subsequent interchanges with you. Just as with your new recipe, you'll improve your ability to communicate assertively a little each time you try it. Your sense of personal worth will also be increased. You will gain courage and confidence.

### Unconfuse the Confused

At first, those with whom you have close relationships might be perplexed by your assertiveness because it's such a change from your previous style. Just as you might have originally confused assertiveness with aggressiveness, others might make the same error. It's very common for both males and females to liken assertion to aggression. Anticipate friends' possible confusion or tendency to overreact. Seize the opportunity to clarify the differences explained in the "Assertive Doesn't Mean Aggressive" section of this chapter.

Carl demonstrated his confusion by overreacting to his wife's very appropriate assertive communication. After serving Pam and Carl dinner in my home, I asked if they would like coffee with dessert. Pam pleasantly requested tea, instead. Before I could oblige, Carl interrupted, "Pam, I've never seen you act so forward. It's not like you to ask for tea when you've been offered coffee."

Ron chuckled, "Well, meet the new me," and explained her goal of becoming a more assertive communicator.

Sylvia's lawyer, Ron, also misidentified assertion as aggression. Sylvia had an appointment with him to sign papers. He never showed for their early afternoon meeting. Calling her at 6:00 P.M., he apologized for having forgotten and requested she come to his downtown office right away. "No, Ron, I can't. Traveling downtown once today has inconvenienced me enough. I know your time is valuable, but so is mine. Please bring the papers by my house on your way home," Sylvia responded politely. "My, aren't you the aggressive one," Ron said, surprised. "No," commented Sylvia, "I'm the assertive one." Ron delivered the papers to Sylvia for her signature.

I, too, must occasionally "debrief" dear friends, who still equate the two vastly different communication styles. My friend Terry, a college president, told me, "I really like talking to you and listening when you speak with others. One never has to read between the lines with you. You say what you think. You are one of the most aggressive women I know." Horrified, I stuttered, "I know you meant it as a compliment, but I'm *not* aggressive, I'm *assertive*." Bewildered, he queried, "What's the difference?" I clarified by providing him with the example described earlier which explains the three possible ways you could react to a cigarette smoker asking permission to smoke in your car. Grinning, Terry replied, "Great example. I see what you mean. I never realized the difference."

Don't be put off by reactions of confusion or surprise at your efforts to communicate assertively. Some people may criticize you or deliberately call you aggressive. Anticipate that this will happen at first so you will be prepared for different reactions. Ultimately, *you* will be the one surprised by the newfound respect and admiration with which people treat you.

## A REPERTOIRE OF RESPONSES

It's time to experiment and try the various communication styles on for size. The purpose is to encourage you to think about and analyze each style. There are no right or wrong answers.

Formulate a submissive, assertive, and aggressive reaction to each of the following situations.

*Situation:* You've been waiting for your car to be serviced at the dealership. Told it's ready, you go outside, prepared to drive away. The car hasn't been washed. The windows and floor mats are filthy. The service manager, handing you the keys, thanks you for your business.

React submissively:

React aggressively:

React assertively:

To compare your three responses with other concrete examples of the different communication styles, I've also formulated three possible reactions to this situation. Do you see similarities between your responses and the samples below?

*Submissive reaction:* Saying, "You're welcome," I accept the car from the service manager. Disappointed because I was looking forward to it being clean and shiny, I drive around looking for a professional car wash.

*Aggressive reaction:* "What kind of low-class outfit is this? This is an outrage. You are incompetent. I want my car cleaned and washed *now.*"

*Assertive reaction:* "Excuse me. I'm sure it was an oversight on your part, but this is completely unacceptable. My windows and floor mats are dirty. I'll be happy to wait a little longer. Please bring me my car when it has been thoroughly washed."

*Situation:* You are extremely annoyed with a colleague who continually addresses you as "honey."

React submissively:

React aggressively.

React assertively:


*Situation:* A client of yours asks you to reduce your customary fee for a service you provide. You know your charges are fair and competitive with the going rate for the same service charged by other professionals in the community.

React submissively:


React aggressively:


React assertively:


*Situation:* You're sitting alone in a crowded theater watching a movie. The loud conversation of a couple near you is disturbing.

React submissively:


React aggressively:


React assertively:


Now, explain the activity to one or more of your friends. Try out your replies on them and ask how they would have reacted in each situation. Ask for their opinions about your different responses.

I had the opportunity to practice assertive communication the first day on the job as a newly appointed dean at a large community college. Another administrator, a rather pushy woman named

Micky, was used to intimidating others to get them to do her bidding. She requested that I allow an extra student into an overcrowded Humanities course. I explained I couldn't because of my policy to respect the wishes of the individual course instructors and allow them to make their own decisions regarding admitting students into already full classes.

It was obvious my explanation was of no interest to her. She was not going to take "no" for an answer. Knowing I had the authority to make the exception and grant her the favor, Micky challenged me, "You *can't* or you *won't?*" I responded in a pleasantly modulated voice, "I won't!" and invited her to directly contact the specific instructor herself. End of discussion. Micky clearly demonstrated her desire to get her way and dominate at my expense. I simply and confidently stated my position. It was clear that submitting to her request was not *my* preference. However, I respected her right to pursue the matter further and make the request directly of the professor. Micky was aggressive; I was assertive. On subsequent occasions, she addressed me in a polite and professional manner. She never again attempted such an intimidation tactic with me. A potentially destructive conflict became productive.

### *Options Provide Power*

Now that you've practiced and learned the different communication styles, you're aware of the options. You're no longer limited to the inhibiting "don't make waves" style which you've used for so long. On the other hand, don't feel obligated to assert yourself if you don't want to. There's more than one appropriate way to act in a given circumstance. The key here is choice. Your choice should be based on how strong your personal feelings are about a particular situation and how you feel at the moment.

I, for one, am usually not annoyed when called "honey" by colleagues, service personnel, and so forth. It's not a sore spot for me. Therefore, I generally have no need to speak up about it. However, it does bother me when someone calls me "honey" in a patronizing or condescending way. My response will depend upon how I feel at the time. I might ignore the comment or respond

Kiiwwurwreiy wiih u vurved evyerkuwuy "It'u *diverur* honey to you!" If being called "honey" or some other term is an issue for you, as it is for many women, responding assertively becomes necessary for you to feel good about yourself.

Terry was not disturbed by Ed's dog barking. Another neighbor, angry about the noise, complained constantly about the problem to Terry. He suggested they confront Ed together. "I have no reason to say anything to Ed, as his dog's barking doesn't annoy me. But, since you find it to be a problem, you should nicely bring it to his attention. I'm sure he'll take care of it," Terry said.

The same remarks or behavior which inconvenience or disturb someone else, might be completely inoffensive to you. In that event, remaining silent is not demonstrating submissiveness—it's your preferred course of action. However, it is important to be honest with yourself. Many women, reluctant to speak up, convince themselves no problem exists when it really does. They talk themselves out of being assertive by claiming not to mind the barking dogs, the rude salesperson, the sloppy repair job, the cold soup, or the bitter coffee. This form of denial is very common. Don't rationalize by telling yourself, "It doesn't bother me" or "It's no big deal" as an excuse to avoid communicating assertively. If you're too inhibited to speak up when you find a situation personally offensive, you deny yourself as a person.

You might deliberately choose not to exercise assertive communication, preferring to initially try a different tactic. Valerie prefers attempting indirect communication to get what she wants from her boss. If that fails, she is fully prepared to follow up using direct, assertive communication. Her department chairman forgot his promise to schedule her to teach a 9:00 A.M. class. Valerie learned through another source he had assigned that time slot to a different instructor. She decided not to bring the actual oversight to his attention. She simply wrote a note reminding him to schedule her for the class. The chairman rectified his error and revised the schedule. It was not necessary for Valerie to pursue the matter further. However, she had every intention of doing so had he not made the adjustment.

You might even decide a strong comeback is the way to go in a particular situation. Beth always referred to Marianne as her "scatterbrained" cousin. Not wanting to upset the applecart, Marianne resented but ignored the put-down for years. Finally, over lunch one day, she laughingly responded to Beth's usual "scatterbrain" put-down: "At least *I* have brains to scatter!"

This somewhat strong reaction was certainly out of character for Marianne. However, she decided to experiment with this type of reply. Marianne consciously delivered it in a playful manner. After considering the options, she made the deliberate decision to respond this way. Fine, it was her choice to make. Some individuals have developed only one communication style, either submissive or aggressive. They have no options. Remain silent if that's really your preference, but speak up for yourself when you want to. Exercise the freedom to choose for yourself how you will act in any given situation.

## Don't Confuse Friend With Foe

A brief word of caution here. Although I strongly advocate firm, swift responses to kill the verbal abuser's attraction to you, take care not to misinterpret the message. If you tend toward a poor self-concept, you might view a harmless remark as an insult or put-down. Instead of swatting at mosquitoes, you might be striking at sweet harmless butterflies without realizing it.

Susana, a rather shy student, was generally reticent about speaking up in class. She finally mustered up the nerve to ask a question during a lecture, and her professor responded by saying, "Now that's an unusual query." She later complained that her professor made her feel self-conscious by his response. She believed he was putting her down by implying that her question was foolish. I was sure this was not his intention and encouraged her to tell him how she felt during his office hours. It turned out that her instructor was genuinely upset that she had misinterpreted his comment. He had intended it as a compliment. He had wanted to acknowledge her display of critical thinking and the insightful question.

Misunderstandings happen to everyone who communicates. They are a fairly regular occurrence. They happen between friends, colleagues, lovers, and family members.

In an article titled "Failure to Communicate a Factor in Air Emergencies" that appeared in the *Washington Post* on February 4, 1990, staff writer Don Phillips wrote:

> Eight days after Avianca Flight 052 crashed into a hillside while circling to land at New York's J.F.K. International Airport, its crew apparently never communicating the seriousness of its fuel shortage, another foreign airliner seemed nervously close to the same fate.
>
> In both the Avianca and LTU (German charter airline) incidents, it seems clear pilots and air traffic controllers had a problem common between husbands and wives, bosses and employees, sergeants and privates: a failure to communicate.

Miscommunication often occurs because listeners assume they know what was meant by the speaker's words. They later blame the speaker as being the source of the problem. (Susana assumed "unusual" meant foolish and that her professor was insulting her.)

Other listeners simply ignore words they don't understand or reject them as contradictory or ridiculous. They never bother to find out what the words mean.

Try this exercise. Read the following paragraph about "Stella."

Stella was level-headed and giddy. She was kind and silly. Stella was tiny but so large that everyone admired her.

What is your opinion of the above paragraph? Did you think the words were contradictory or made no sense? Did you call the author crazy? Well, with our everyday meaning of words, this message does sound like nonsense. However, in the early English language, many of the words had completely different meanings.

*Giddy* meant enthusiastic or divinely possessed. It was derived from the same stem as God.

*Silly* meant happy. It came from the German word "soelig."

*Large* referred to a good-hearted or generous person.

If you substitute what the words mean today, you have the following:

> Stella was level-headed and enthusiastic. She was kind and happy. Stella was tiny but so generous everyone admired her.

Now that the words make sense, you won't reject them or call them nonsense. You will no longer criticize the author. If people made a consistent effort to clarify what other people say to them, misunderstandings would occur less frequently. Listeners need to say to themselves, "I don't understand the message. I better ask some questions about it. It might mean something different to someone else."

Before you assume someone's well-intentioned statement is a put-down, be sure you haven't misinterpreted what was meant. Ask yourself, "Have I really been insulted?" Often, this is a simple matter of asking, "What did you mean by that?" This will go a long way toward avoiding feelings of ill will that frequently come between friends due to a misunderstanding.

Peggy was expecting a delivery and knew she would not be home to accept it. She requested that the delivery people leave the parcel with her neighbor, Anne, who was pleased to do her friend the favor. Anne brought the small package to Peggy's home after dinner. Peggy exclaimed, "I'm sure glad you didn't know what was in the box. Those are the diamond earrings my daughter sent for my birthday."

Anne's first reaction was to feel slighted and assume that her honesty was being impugned. She was upset and surprised, knowing that insulting others was not her neighbor's style. However, she realized she should double-check her interpretation. "Why are you glad I didn't know what was in the box?" she asked. Peggy immediately replied, "Because, had you known, you might have been unwilling to accept such a valuable package." Anne was extremely relieved to learn that Peggy hadn't meant to imply that she was untrustworthy.

When you suspect a speaker's remarks are dishonorable or meant to demean, requesting clarification serves another useful purpose, it frequently breaks that person of the habit of engaging in put-down conduct—at least with *you!*

Clyde, the chairman of a committee comprised of five males and one female (Judy), needed to have the minutes recorded at a meeting. He looked at the group and commented, "That's a skirt job. Let Judy do it." Knowing full well he meant a task typically delegated to females (taking notes, buying Christmas presents, changing diapers, etc.), Judy pleasantly intoned, "Gee, Clyde, I'm unfamiliar with that term. What do you mean by a 'skirt job'?" Clyde, too embarrassed to have to spell out such a blatantly chauvinistic term in front of the others, mumbled, "Never mind. I'll take the minutes myself."

Of course, asking Clyde what he meant might not have embarrassed him at all. If he were a complete Neanderthal, he might simply have explained the meaning of the term and laughed. After all, some numbskulls won't get a subtle hint. They think that their idiotic remarks are oh-so-clever and so they will continue making them. In that case, you need a somewhat stronger response.

Carrie, my editor, calls this technique "escalating" one's responses. Here's how it works. Suppose Judy's gentle request for clarification didn't solve the problem. She could "escalate" her response and deliver a humorous but more resolute one, such as, "Oh, what a quaint term. I can see somebody's still living in the past!" And if that still didn't work, an even more forceful tact might have been to speak to Clyde privately and say, "That's a rather chauvinistic expression. I'm not real keen on doing jobs you consider *skirt jobs.* Okay?" To show that she harbored no ill will toward Clyde for his "skirt job" comment, Judy could even add, "By the way, would you like to have lunch next week to discuss the new marketing plan?"

Directly requesting clarification might even help you end a potentially uncomfortable situation before it begins. Lorena, a former student of mine, called me a year after having taken one of my classes. She described how this technique helped her avoid a potentially explosive situation. Mr. Meyer, the branch manager of the bank where she was a teller, approached her, commenting, "I would like to have a relationship with you." Lorena mildly asserted, "Thank you. I think we have a very nice working relationship right now." "That's not what I meant," Mr. Myer countered. Lorena *escalated* her response, "Well, Mr. Meyer, I believe in the importance of avoiding possible miscommunications because so many words have more than one meaning. Just so there is no misunderstanding, why don't you clarify exactly what you meant by *relationship*?" The manager wisely took the hint and made no further advances.

Both Judy and Lorena resolved their situations easily and effectively with gentle assertions. Of course, there's no guarantee that similar scenarios will have such happy endings. However, you've got nothing to lose and everything to gain by starting with a mild request for clarification. It sure beats becoming indignant or having to scream "sexual harassment" if you don't have to.

As you can see, clarifying to avoid a misunderstanding is necessary. It may even stimulate the verbal sadists and self-esteem robbers to rethink their behavior and treat you as an equal. Demonstrating the willingness to directly seek verification of a speaker's motives is an important step in becoming verbally fit.

Once you've determined a speaker's intentions were not honorable and the remark was, in fact, a "dig," you must reply. Your self-respect depends upon it. Even a simple "That remark was uncalled for and I don't appreciate it" can make you feel like a million bucks because it lets others know that you value yourself as a person. And that's the real payoff here—to show that you respect your own self!

## The Road to Reform

It's worth mentioning there are those who truly don't realize how humiliating their remarks can be. Some individuals are not necessarily ill-intentioned. They are simply unaware that their comments are hurtful to others. Displaying insensitivity toward others' rights has become an automatic behavior for them. Once made aware of the situation, many people remedy it appropriately. Although a lot of put-down artists know full well what they're doing, some really are oblivious to the damage they inflict. Many will react responsively when a problem is brought to their attention. Politely pointing out hurtful cracks might be just what is needed to start them on the road to reform. They might truly value their relationship with you and want to change to preserve it.

Gary Smalley, a well-known author and speaker on personal and family relationships, tells how he unwittingly "wounded his wife's spirit." In his *Hidden Keys to Loving Relationships* video series, he describes how he used to demean his wife, Norma, without realizing it. He says,

> When we were first married, I used to tell a lot of jokes when I spoke to young people's groups. Norma would go with me and I'd say, "Let me introduce my wife, Norma. She treats me like a God. Every morning she serves me burnt offerings." Or I'd say, "The other day she and I took a trip. At the airport, the skycap came out and asked if he could help me with my bag. I said 'No thanks. She can walk.'" I thought my jokes were a scream. The problem is, I was unaware what that was doing to my wife. I had no idea that doing that kind of thing can deeply offend and close the spirit of someone.

Fortunately, Norma told Gary how she felt and that she didn't appreciate the "funny jokes." Once it was brought to his attention, Gary was willing and able to change his hurtful behavior.

I, myself, have been pleasantly surprised to receive sincere apologies from individuals who were inadvertently jeopardizing our relationship by making insensitive remarks or jokes at my expense. It has been very gratifying to hear, "I'm sorry, I really didn't mean any harm," "I didn't realize how I sounded," "I wish you had told me sooner so I could have done something before now," or "I'll be more careful in the future. Thanks for telling me." Insensitive communicators deserve a chance to change. Give them one. If they don't take advantage of your generosity, then *they* become the losers. Bear in mind, people will treat you the way you teach them to treat you.

Your response should be polite but firm enough to have the desired effect. If it is too weak, the abuser might not be deterred.

Marcia frequently interrupted Robin and told her to "shut up." Robin mildly protested each time without result. At a book club discussion, Marcia told her to "shut up" again. Robin decided that her usually mild protest needed to be "escalated" to get Marcia to change her behavior. She replied in a clear, firm voice, "Marcia, your behavior is unacceptable. Please don't cut me off and tell me to 'shut up.' I know you want to express your opinions, but it's my turn to speak. There's time for both of us to be heard." Marcia sincerely apologized, "I get so caught up in what I want to say, I forget about everyone else, I'm really sorry." A lively, enjoyable discussion about the book ensued.

As you can see, Robin protected her right to express herself without interruption while acknowledging Marcia's need to be heard. Robin orchestrated a win-win situation with her assertive communication.

In their book *Women and the Art of Negotiating,* authors Juliet Nierenberg and Irene Ross have this to say about "the Bully":

> The bully has found that, with some people, his behavior gets results. But take a look at him with those people he can't manipulate and it's like looking at a different person. He's respectful, doesn't make unreasonable or excessive demands, and doesn't try to intimidate. Why? Because the people he respects wouldn't submit to his bullying stance. Because they have demanded a different relationship, they have established one based on reason.

Although your verbal fitness will be its own reward, it will lead to many other benefits. When you no longer permit people to take advantage of you, they will respect you more for standing up for yourself. You will no longer feel powerless or personally insignificant. You will respect yourself and feel an intoxicating liberation. You will find that more often than not, situations go your way. Your assertiveness might even be the catalyst needed to set verbal abusers on the "road to reform." It will give insensitive communicators a chance to respond appropriately and even change the behavior that triggered your assertiveness in the first place. Remember, assertive does not mean aggressive. Experiment with a variety of responses until you find the ones that work best for you. Be sure to clarify the speaker's intentions to avoid miscommunications. And, keep in mind, one politely assertive response is worth one thousand ineffective, submissive ones.

Go for it! Be unappealing to users and abusers by becoming a verbally fit and assertive communicator.

# 2

# *Adopt Assertive Speech and Body Language*

Haley is a tall, intelligent, and extremely attractive thirty-five-year-old computer programmer. However, because of the way she speaks, people often don't take her seriously.

Haley recently bought an expensive pair of shoes at a large department store. After wearing them twice, both heels fell off. She finally took them back to the store for a refund after procrastinating for two weeks about whether or not she should. With her shoulders slouched, her body stooped, and her head hung toward the floor, she timidly approached a salesclerk. Every sentence she spoke sounded like a question. "Uh, excuse me? I'm, uh, sorry to be, um, such a bother? But, uh, the heels fell off these shoes? I was hoping you could, uh, refund my purchase price?" The salesclerk impatiently responded, "The manager has to authorize all refunds." Still looking down, Haley nervously twirled a strand of hair around her finger. "Well, um, if it's not too inconvenient, uh, would it be okay if I, um, showed him these shoes and, uh, asked for a refund?" The clerk snapped, "He's busy right now. You'll have to wait." Feeling discouraged, Haley just left.

Posture, eye contact, facial expressions, and gestures make up body language. Your body language, as well as your speech patterns, reflects how you feel about yourself and affects how others react to you. Body language and speech patterns can help you convey an aura of confidence and high self-esteem or make you appear indecisive and unsure before you even open your mouth. William Shakespeare wrote that all speakers give two speeches at the same time: the one that is heard and the one that is seen. When your posture, gestures, and expressions don't match your spoken message, people will believe your body language message. For example, if someone introduced to you says "It's so nice to meet you" but she rolls her eyes and isn't smiling, she's sending you a mixed message. Her words are saying "It's nice to meet you" but her body language is saying something else.

A professor at UCLA found that only 7 percent of our credibility with listeners comes from the actual words we speak while 38 percent comes from our vocal qualities. He found that an amazing 55 percent of our believability comes from our visual characteristics. The presidential debates between John F. Kennedy and Richard Nixon in 1960 are an excellent example of how facial expressions, gestures, eye contact, and posture can hurt speakers or help them get their message across. These debates were the first ever to be televised. The people who heard them on the radio said that Nixon won the debates. But the people who watched them on TV insisted that Kennedy won. Kennedy's visual qualities were much better than Nixon's. Kennedy's body language made a more powerful impression on the viewers than anything the candidates were actually saying.

Haley clearly didn't know how to use assertive speech and body language. Doing so would have helped her develop courage and confidence. Unlike Haley, you'll find that others will pay attention to you and accept the words you say when you make an effort to improve your posture and use of gestures, look your listeners in the eye, and use assertive and decisive-sounding speech patterns.

### *Posture Talks*

Your posture shows how you feel about yourself. It sends one of two messages to the world at large. It can say, "I'm timid and afraid of my own shadow. Don't listen to me; just ignore me. I don't respect myself. You don't need to respect me either." On the other hand, your posture can send the message, "Listen to me. I know what I'm talking about. I know what I need and want. I expect to be treated with the respect I deserve. I'm not subservient to you; we're equal!"

Haley's posture, with her slouched shoulders and head hung toward the floor, conveyed the first message. Looking down and refusing to face people directly gives the impression you're ashamed or embarrassed. Cocking your head to the side, rounding your shoulders, dropping your chin, clutching your arms across your shoulders, wrapping your arms around your body, or clasping your hands tightly in front of you makes you appear insecure and defeated. It tells listeners that you lack confidence and don't expect to be taken seriously.

I'm sure you'd prefer to convey a positive message. There are several ways you can radiate confidence and strength of character, even before you open your mouth!

- Keep your spine straight and rotate your shoulders back.
- Keep your head erect.
- Keep your hands at your sides with your fingers open or slightly curled.
- Keep both feet flat on the floor a shoulder's width apart.

You can also project a confident posture when you're sitting and listening.

- Sit straight while leaning forward slightly to show interest in the speaker.
- Rest your hands lightly in your lap or on the arms of your chair.
- Keep your legs together with your feet flat on the floor or crossed at the ankles.

Observe the body language of the women in figure 2–1. Who looks the most confident and self-assured? If you said Cheryl, you're right on target. What is it about Cheryl's posture that causes her to project courage and confidence?

Susan          Tanya          Cheryl          Jill

Figure 2–1.

Improving your posture isn't difficult. It's as simple as doing what your mother probably used to tell you all the time: "Stand up straight," "Stop slouching," or "Sit up in your chair!" Haitian women in Haiti have the best posture in the world. They walk for miles carrying baskets of fruits and vegetables on their heads. The good news is that you won't need baskets of produce to improve your posture! The old finishing-school trick of walking around your house with a book on your head still works wonders. Practice balancing a book on your head while sitting in a chair or walking from room to room. Pretend an invisible string is holding your head up. Rotate your shoulders back and balance that book!

### Look Them in the Eyes

Making eye contact with your listeners is absolutely essential for becoming verbally fit. Looking your listeners directly in their eyes can be more effective than the words you say. It forces them to pay attention to you, respond to you, and to respect you. When you avoid eye contact, people get the impression you are anxious, dishonest, embarrassed, or ashamed. The right amount of eye contact indicates that you have confidence in yourself and what you're saying. It shows that you respect yourself and expect to be acknowledged as an equal.

Haley lacks self-confidence and feels inferior to others. Her failure to look the salesclerk in the eye sent a powerful message. It said, "I'm not as important as you are. I don't expect you to take me seriously." And, if you recall, the salesclerk in the department store barely paid any attention to Haley.

The thought of maintaining eye contact with someone may be disconcerting to you at first. That's a perfectly normal reaction. It may be helpful for you to keep in mind that effective eye contact doesn't mean you should constantly stare into someone's eyes.

The next time you're conversing with someone, try this exercise:

1. Focus on one of the person's eyes for four seconds.
2. Shift your focus to their other eye for four seconds.
3. Now look at the person's entire face for four seconds.
4. Glance at the nose for four seconds, the chin for four seconds, and the forehead for four seconds.
5. Continue to alternate between focusing on each eye for four seconds, the whole face for four seconds, and the nose, forehead, and chin for four seconds each.

Practice these steps in any conversational situation. You will be amazed at how self-assured and comfortable you become.

### Are You Asking Me or Telling Me?

This is a declarative sentence? The way some people speak, it may as well be!

Your voice has a natural upward inflection when you ask a question, as in, "Would you like coffee?" If you use the upward inflection too much, however, you'll sound insecure and unsure of yourself. "Uptalk" turns comments into questions even if you are not asking anything! Haley's voice had an indefinite, tentative quality. She made her statements sound like questions. "Excuse me? I'm sorry to be such a bother? The heels fell off these shoes? I was hoping you could refund my purchase price?" This uptalk made Haley sound like a person who had no faith in herself. If she had spoken in an assertive way, "Excuse *me*. I'd appreciate your *help*. The heels fell off these *shoes*. I'd like a *refund*," she would have sounded more confident. In addition, she probably would have been treated with respect and gotten her refund.

Sally was twenty-eight years old and was a new math teacher at a large junior high school. She had problems disciplining her students and was not as effective a teacher as she knew she could be. At lunch one day, she discussed her problem with Judd, the speech teacher. After observing her teach a lesson, Judd diagnosed the problem. Her students frequently ignored her instructions. She always sounded like she was asking rather than telling her students to do assignments. "Do the exercises on page thirty-five for homework?" "Study your formulas for the quiz Tuesday?"

Judd helped Sally get rid of her uptalk. Once she learned to drop the pitch of her voice at the end of sentences, her students began to take her seriously. They realized that she meant what she said.

Why ask when you can tell! People won't listen to you if your voice turns every sentence into a question. Why should they? Using an upward inflection at the end of your statements tells your listeners, "Don't pay attention to me. I don't know what I'm talking about." After all, how much faith would you have in a doctor who says, "Your wrist isn't sprained? It's broken? I need to operate?"

Let's say you're selling your car and the prospective buyer asks for your best price. If you tentatively answer, "Six thousand?" the buyer will know you can be bargained down. But if you respond *"Six thousand"* in a confident tone with a downward intonation, the buyer will know that your asking price is firm.

Remember, an upward intonation signals a question and a falling pitch signals a statement. "It's raining?" "It's raining!" In the written form, punctuation marks tell us the first is a question and the second is a statement. When spoken, the listener knows that the first is a question because it is said with the speaker's voice going up at the end. The second "It's raining" is said with a downward intonation. If you use uptalk for declarative statements, you'll sound uncertain and reduce the value of your ideas.

The following exercises will help you practice dropping your pitch at the end of statements and eliminate uptalk from your speech.

*Exercise 1.* Say each of the following statements twice. Use a falling pitch to end the statement in the first column. Then, in column 2, use an upward pitch to turn the same statement into a question. (Notice how the falling pitch helps you sound sure of yourself while the rising pitch makes you sound doubtful or uncertain.)

| *State with conviction!* | *State with doubt?* |
| --- | --- |
| We need a better filing system! | We need a better filing system? |
| I'm going to succeed at this job! | I'm going to succeed at this job? |
| I deserve a promotion! | I deserve a promotion? |
| I'm due for a raise! | I'm due for a raise? |
| I'm a good teacher! | I'm a good teacher? |

*Exercise 2.* Enlist the aid of a friend or family member. Explain what uptalk is and tell her that your goal is to get rid of it. Whenever you end a sentence as if it were a question, ask her to stop you by saying "uptalk" or some other "code word." I bet your uptalk will become extinct within two weeks!

## Discard Those Disclaimers

Too many women use disclaimers or apologize for their comments before they even make them! Disclaimers are remarks that weaken or diminish the impact of what the speaker is about to say. They can kill good ideas before they're born!

The managers at General Foods encourage their employees to express their ideas freely and confidently. They tell them not to preface their remarks with "idea killing phrases" such as:

This probably won't work, but...
This isn't too practical, but...
This may not work here, but let me tell you anyway...
Here's an idea, for what it's worth...

I'm not sure I like this idea myself, but...

This may sound screwy to you, but maybe there's some way
we can use it...

I'd like to go over this for a minute or two, even at the risk of
boring you....*

Speakers who use disclaimers and apologies when they speak
sound unsure of themselves. Other common disclaimers include:

I could be wrong, but...
I'm not sure, but...
I may be way off track, but...
I might have misunderstood, but...
This is probably a dumb idea, but...
I know I ask too many questions, but...
I'm not an expert on this, but...
I don't know much about this topic, but....

Comments like these reduce your credibility with listeners. They
belittle you and diminish the value of your opinions and feelings.
Haley let the salesclerk know she considered herself to be a pest
and not worthy of assistance by prefacing her request with, "I'm
sorry to be such a bother, but...." Avoid these types of remarks.
Speak your mind without first apologizing or disclaiming your
words.

The following statements are full of apologies and disclaimers.
Turn each one into a confident sounding, assertive statement.
Follow the first pair as an example.

*Apology:* I know I don't know much about CD players, but shouldn't
we comparison shop before making a purchase?

*Assertive Statement:* We should comparison shop before we buy a
new CD player.

*Apology:* I'm sorry for asking so many questions, but could you
please explain the difference between these two CD players?

---

*From *Speaker's Sourcebook II*

*Assertive Statement:*


*Apology:* I know I haven't worked for the organization as long as some of the other employees, but I hope you'll consider me for the promotion.

*Assertive Statement:*


*Apology:* This may be a stupid question, but are we going to a have a final exam in this course?

*Assertive Statement:*


*Apology:* This probably won't work, but we might bring in more customers and increase sales by offering senior citizens a 15 percent discount.

*Assertive Statement:*


*Apology:* I know I don't know much about displaying merchandise, but I think this display would look better if it were moved to the front of the store.

*Assertive Statement:*


### Silence Is Golden

You know? You know what I mean? Um! Er! Uh! These distracting expressions and noises are called vocal fillers. They distract from your message and signal others that you're uneasy. Haley was so unsure of herself that she filled every pause with an "um" or "uh." "Uh. Excuse me? I'm, uh, sorry to be, um, such a bother? But, uh, the heels fell off these shoes? I was, um, hoping you could, uh, refund my purchase price?" These fillers in Haley's speech were extremely distracting and caused her to appear even more nervous and insecure than she actually was.

Assertive, confident speakers know the importance of deliberate silences when they speak. Speakers who use well-placed pauses and avoid vocal fillers are regarded as being more confident and knowledgeable than speakers who don't. For some reason, we are uneasy with silence and feel that every second needs to be filled with sound. Well, it doesn't. Silence can be golden. There's nothing wrong with a few seconds of silence while you are thinking of what you want to say next. There's nothing wrong with a moment of silence if you temporarily forget what you want to say. Brief silences or pauses between your comments give you and your listeners time to think and time to consider what you've just said.

In *Speak With Power and Grace,* speech expert Linda D. Swink writes, "I firmly believe the first two words in the English language are 'Well, ah!' Watch any TV news program or game show when the reporter or host asks a question. You'll notice the person responding will begin by saying, 'Well, ah.' And the 'ahs' don't stop there; they are peppered throughout our speech unknowingly. Filler words are distracting, annoying, and unprofessional."

So don't feel the need to fill every pause with unnecessary vocal fillers. Learn to feel comfortable with brief silences between your thoughts and ideas.

The following exercises will help you eliminate distracting vocal fillers and make your speech flow smoothly.

1. Enlist the aid of friends or family members. Explain that your goal is to get rid of distracting speech habits. Ask them to let you know whenever they hear you say "you know," "um," "er," or "uh" while you're speaking.
2. Record yourself while having a conversation with a friend on the telephone or in person. Record yourself telling a joke or describing an interesting experience you had. Then listen to yourself and analyze how you sound. Become aware of any distracting vocal habits you might have. Do you use uptalk or disclaimers? Do you use annoying vocal fillers instead of silences in your speech? The sooner you're able to eliminate ineffective vocal habits, the sooner you'll develop more assertive, confident sounding speech.

3. Think of any simple topic or subject such as apples, pens, rocks, ties, jewelry, chairs, anything you like. Then record yourself speaking off the top of your head about that topic for 60 seconds. Your goal is to speak fluently without the use of *long* pauses, hesitations, or vocal fillers. Listen to your recording. Did you fill every pause with sound (*you know, um, er, uh*), or were you able to use silence instead? Practice this until you can speak continuously for at least 60 seconds about a topic. This will help you gain confidence in your ability to speak fluently and assertively.

### Less Is More

My colleague Jane is not an insecure woman, but she sure sounds like' one at times. She, like many women, often feels an overwhelming need to justify her response to questions with lengthy explanations. Here's an example.

Jane and I were invited to the downtown Miami Hyatt Regency Hotel for a working luncheon related to college business. As we pulled up to the entrance, the parking valet asked, "Are you staying at the hotel?" Jane immediately began, "No, not exactly. You see, we're administrators at Miami Dade Community College and we've been invited to have lunch because we're on the planning committee to organize the reception at the inauguration which is going to be held here for our new district president. I don't know how long we'll be here exactly, but it shouldn't be more than a couple of hours...."

"Excuse me ma'am," the valet interrupted. "I just wanted to know if you were staying at the hotel."

As the valet drove off in her car, Jane turned to me sheepishly, "I don't know why I didn't simply say, 'No, we're just here for lunch.' You'd think I was afraid he was going to throw me out if I didn't justify why I was here." "Oh, forget it," I laughed. "You just gave me a great example for the 'Less Is More' section of my book!"

People who lack self-confidence often feel compelled to provide lengthy justifications for their behavior. Furthermore, they often feel they have to provide a plethora of reasons to support every statement they make. Women who do this come across as being timid and unsure of themselves.

Carol was a freelance management consultant. A client was long overdue in paying his bill. When Carol finally called him to request payment, she meekly began with an apology, "I'm sorry to bother you but I really need you to send my check as soon as possible. You see, my daughter's going away to college and needs a new car and my son's college tuition is due next week and...."

Whoa! What's wrong with this picture? I see plenty wrong. First of all, Carol has no cause to apologize for bothering her client. He should apologize for not paying his bill on time. Second of all, Carol doesn't owe him a list of reasons why she should be paid her fee. It's none of the client's business that her daughter needs a new car and her son's college tuition payment is due. Carol has every right to be paid for her services and needn't justify why! Carol might have exercised assertive communication with her client by saying, "I prepared a management plan for your company two months ago. Your payment is overdue. I'd appreciate receiving your check for services rendered as soon as possible."

The value of keeping remarks succinct without unnecessary clarification has inspired a variety of sayings throughout history:

Let thy speech be short, comprehending much in few words.
    (Ancient Greek philosopher)
Brevity is the soul of wit. (William Shakespeare)
I have never been hurt by anything I didn't say. (Calvin Coolidge)
Talk low, talk slow, and don't say too much. (John Wayne)
Many people who have the gift of gab don't know how to
    wrap it up. (Arnold Glasow)
The less said the better. (Popular expression)

Both men and women would do well to keep these quotes in mind while speaking!

More often than not, our well-intentioned dissertations are clearly unnecessary. We get so distracted by the desire to explain ourselves, we don't realize our listeners aren't interested in the extra verbiage, and that it's actually hurting our cause. Consider the following exchange between Linda and a cashier in an electronics store.

Cashier: What's your mailing address?
Linda: I'd rather not give it because…
Cashier: Fine. No problem.
Linda: Every time I give my address to a store, I end up on another mailing list. I really don't want to receive any more junk mail so I hope you don't mind that I don't want to give you…
Cashier: Excuse me. It's okay. You don't have to give me your address if you don't want to!

Jane, Carol, and Linda all felt the need to support their actions with superfluous explanations. Assertive, confident-sounding speakers avoid the temptation to unnecessarily justify their behavior or responses. So, when you find yourself in a situation where you're tempted to explain yourself to the *nth* degree, step on the brakes. Remind yourself of the popular expression, "The less said the better!"

### *Simply Say "Thank You"*

I used to have a hard time accepting compliments until a college psychology professor taught me a valuable lesson. He complimented me on a presentation I made in class. Wrinkling my nose as if disgusted, I muttered, "It wasn't as good as some of the others." My professor shouted, "Stop! Analyze what just happened. I gave you a present and you threw it on the floor!" As I began to apologize, he continued. "You must learn to accept compliments gracefully. Try saying a simple 'Thank you' next time."

Many women have a difficult time accepting direct compliments. They become embarrassed and try to brush the compliment off with some self-deprecating remark. When praised for their appearance, personality, or clothing, I've heard women make such comments as:

You can't be serious.
I have much nicer dresses than this old rag.
This haircut makes my nose look big.
If you think I'm fun to be with, you don't know me very well.
You need glasses. I'm fat as a house.
My outfit has been out of style for years.

Unlike men, who readily accept credit for their success, women often become uncomfortable when praised for what they've done. They tend to devalue compliments about their achievements with such remarks as:

It was nothing.
Anybody could have done it.
It isn't anything special.
I got lucky, that's all.
I just had a good day.

In the beauty salon one afternoon, I overheard Carmen, a stylist, compliment her client on a necklace. "That's so pretty, Dolly." Dolly's response? "You must be kidding. It's just cheap junk. I bought it at the flea market." Carmen's face fell.

When people tell you that you're special, or you look nice, or you've done a good job, accept their remarks with an assertive "Thank you." Tossing the praise off, as Dolly did, makes complimentors feel as if they have shown poor judgment. You're attacking their opinions and observations of you. Remember, comments that discount the compliment tend to discount the compliment giver. Dolly's comments were actually insulting to Carmen. Confident, assertive communicators accept direct compliments without downplaying or ridiculing the compliments with belittling remarks.

The next time you feel uncomfortable when someone pays you a compliment and you begin to deny it, try the following techniques:

• Step on the brakes. Stop yourself, as my professor stopped me. Talk to yourself before responding. Tell yourself, "This person has paid me a compliment. I should feel good about it, not embarrassed. Anyway, I should make him glad he compli-

mented me, not sorry!" Acknowledge the compliment gracefully and assertively with one of the following:

Thank you very much.
Thanks. What a nice thing to say.
I appreciate that. Thank you.

- Try this after you're able to comfortably and assertively accept
  compliments with a simple "Thank you." After gracefully
  acknowledging a compliment, add a remark of your own.

  Complimentor: That was a great dinner.
  You: Thank you. I tried a new recipe. I'm so glad you liked it.

  Complimentor: You took off a lot of weight and look lovely.
  You: Thank you for noticing. It wasn't easy losing thirty pounds.

  Complimentor: You did a great job on the annual report.
  You: Thank you very much. I worked hard to revise the for-
    mat I used last year.

Make sure your body language is in synch with your words of
appreciation. Accepting a compliment gracefully involves four
simple steps:

1. Hold your head high.
2. Look the person in the eye.
3. Smile.
4. Say, "Thank you."

Practice these steps while looking in the mirror. You'll soon be
accepting compliments with style and grace!

A good exercise to help you develop an assertive appearance
involves the use of a full-length mirror. You can become aware of
how you look to others by experimenting with your body language
and facial expressions. Look at yourself and see what others see
when you do the following:

**BODY LANGUAGE**

1. Cover your mouth with your hand while speaking.
2. Sway back and forth on your feet.

3. Cross your arms in front of you.
4. Wrap your arms around your body.
5. Tilt your head.
6. Twirl a strand of your hair around your finger.
7. Play with a button or item of jewelry.
8. Shake your head excessively while speaking.
9. Cross your legs.
10. Look down at your feet.

## FACIAL EXPRESSIONS

1. Smile at yourself.
2. Look worried.
3. Wrinkle your eyebrows.
4. Look interested.
5. Squint your eyes.
6. Bite your lip or lick your lips.
7. Frown at yourself.
8. Scowl at yourself.
9. Look unhappy.
10. Look neutral.

Assertive speech and body language enhance the effect of your words and give your message an impact that words alone don't have. They will make your listeners pay attention to you and more readily accept what you have to say. You now realize that it's not always what you say but how you say it that really matters. Say "no" to uptalk, disclaimers, vocal fillers, and lengthy explanations. Say "yes" to good posture and eye contact, and accept direct compliments. Remember, your speech patterns and body language talk. What they say is up to you!

# 3

# *Prepare for Confrontation*

Blanca, a Certified Public Accountant for a Health Maintenance Organization (HMO), was called to a meeting with several of the physicians and the owner of a medical billing firm. As she entered the room, Dr. Carlon, the HMO administrator, introduced her, "This is Blanca, our billing girl." Blanca replied, smiling, "Just for the record, I'm the CPA for the organization, but I feel like the billing girl half the time!" Although Blanca's assertion was clearly appropriate and pleasant, Dr. Carlon belligerently uttered, "Begging her majesty's pardon, it must be her time of the month."

You must be prepared for the possibility of confrontation. Some may react with disbelief as you begin to speak up for the first time. They may feel threatened by your newly assertive communication style. These people have their own agendas and won't gracefully accept a courteous but clearly assertive response from you. They may respond aggressively in an effort to intimidate you back into submission. They might try to make you feel guilty or selfish for insisting that your wants, needs, and desires are respected. Others will act as though you have victimized them, or they will use your assertive reply as an excuse to further criticize you. Don't allow your emerging confidence and efforts to communicate directly and assertively to be undermined by anyone. Don't back down.

Difficult people will soon learn they can't decrease your self-esteem to increase their own. They will eventually change their behavior as a result of the limits you've clearly set.

Much has been written about the differences in men's and women's communications styles. In *You Just Don't Understand: Men and Women in Conversation,* author Deborah Tannen, Ph.D., a pioneer in the field, writes, "People who are not afraid of conflict have an advantage in innumerable inevitable situations where others try to get their way. Many women learn to avoid confrontation in order to get along with people and be liked." Dr. Tannen points out that this avoidance of conflict leaves them wide open for exploitation because they don't stand up for themselves. Even celebrity women are not immune. Tannen quotes Oprah Winfrey as having said,

> My biggest flaw is my inability to confront people. After all the shows I've done, the books I've read, the psychologists I've talked to, I still allow myself to get ripped off to the nth degree. It takes me days of procrastinating and agonizing before I can work up the nerve to say anything. Sometimes I think I'd rather just run out and get hit by a truck than confront someone who is ripping me off.

Dr. Tannen summarizes, "This is not Oprah Winfrey's idiosyncratic flaw; it is a problem that innumerable women experience."

I know that dealing with hostility and criticism becomes a trying emotional experience. It is natural to want to avoid confrontation. However, even if the result of your appropriate assertive communication is unpleasant, remember how helpless and unhappy the alternative makes you feel. Remaining silent just to avoid rocking the boat is even worse. Resist the temptation to return to your passive style of keeping quiet in order to keep the peace. In the long run, giving in or denying your feelings takes a far greater emotional toll on you than dealing with confrontation every now and then. Be assured that verbal abusers will adjust to the newly assertive you in short order. By taking a firm stand, you will maintain your dignity and discourage their inappropriate behavior.

Interestingly, confrontations with people actually have benefits.

They allow you to get closer to individuals and work to resolve problems instead of ignoring them. The sooner you assert yourself with a difficult person, the more confident you'll feel. When you speak up for yourself, you increase your self-esteem and feel energized. In *Working Women's Communications Survival Guide,* author Ruth Siress states, "Every conflict provides an opportunity for growth, an opportunity to energize a relationship. The opposite of love is apathy, not hate. As long as there is conflict in a relationship, there is energy to work on it. Once apathy has set in, it may be too late."

So please—don't fear confrontation or conflict. Rather than attempt to avoid it, look at it as an opportunity to improve a relationship. Continue to display the confidence that will allow you to say what you think anytime, anywhere. Keep in mind, however, there are many who will be disconcerted by your assertive communication, however mild and pleasant. Confronters will attempt to strike back in a number of ways to keep you from changing. Just be prepared for a variety of different reactions and you will prevail.

## *"You Must Be Suffering From PMS"*

Aggressive confronters are concerned you are showing spunk and protesting their need for ego satisfaction at your expense. These belligerent characters would like to believe your display of assertive communication is a fluke, as they much prefer your previously submissive style. In an effort to "send you back where you came from," they are likely to strike back with such statements as:

Bitch!
Look, the doggie is barking back.
Oh, she must be suffering from PMS.
You must be having a bad day.
She probably hasn't had sex in a while.
Don't take out your frustrations on me, lady.

It takes a lot of willpower to ignore these remarks. However, by turning your back and refusing to dignify an obnoxious statement, you'll be rewarded with terrific feelings of confidence and self-respect.

Only *you* can decide whether it's appropriate to continue interacting with an aggressive confrontor. Blanca decided to quit while she was ahead and ignore Dr. Carlon's sexist comment about it being "her time of the month." She pleasantly asserted herself, made her point, and gained the respect of those present.

Trish, a bookkeeper, handled herself a bit differently in an altercation with Meredith. Meredith, the office manager at a large company, enjoyed demeaning various employees by habitually saying, "What's wrong with you. You look like a deer in the headlights!" Even though Trish knew that this referred to a deer paralyzed with fear upon looking into the headlights of an oncoming vehicle, she used the "request for clarification" technique. One time, after Meredith accused her of looking like a deer in the headlights, Trish said, "Meredith, I don't know what that means. Please be kind enough to explain." Meredith responded aggressively. "You can't be that stupid, Trish. Even my eight-year-old daughter knows what that means." Trish decided to "escalate" her response before walking away. She turned and calmly said, "I'm sure she would. You use the expression so frequently!"

Your goal is not necessarily to continue a verbal Ping-Pong match with the confrontor. When your direct no-nonsense communication evokes such hostility, as it did in Trish's and Blanca's case, you know you've it your mark. It may be time to turn your back and walk away. The best way to deal with such a confrontor may be to ignore the immature reaction. The verbal abuser has already demeaned themself in the eyes of others by displaying this childish behavior. An additional rejoinder on your part may just confirm that his/her remarks got to you.

Of course, it is often difficult to resist a clever retort if one occurs to you, as it did with Trish. Several clever comebacks appropriate for use in a variety of situations are suggested in chapter 8: "Don't Put Up With Put-Downs." If returning the challenge by "trading a quip for a quip" would increase your sense of personal power, I'm all for it. It's your call. Remember, options provide power.

*Choosing* not to respond is not the same as being *unable* to respond. As long as you are confident you could assert yourself if you wanted to, choosing not to is a perfectly healthy choice. Blanca could have retorted, "That was very inappropriate, Dr. Carlon. Please refrain from such remarks in the future." But she chose not to. You must use your judgment and decide if it's appropriate in your particular situation. Remain steadfast in asserting yourself on future occasions with the same individuals. Their abuses might not stop completely, but you will maintain your self-respect in the face of derogatory comments.

### *"I Was Counting on Your Support"*

People who expect to be catered to are notorious for laying guilt trips on those who refuse to do their bidding or follow their preconceived agenda. They will make every effort to shame you through guilt into fulfilling their needs and expectations. When you object or say no to their request, don't be surprised to hear:

I can't believe you won't help me.
I thought for sure you'd want to help such a worthy cause.
You're the last person I expected to turn me down.
But I was counting on you.
It will be just a minor inconvenience but it means so much to me.

Cindy, an insurance agent, was asked for the fifth consecutive year to coordinate contributions for the company's annual United Way campaign. Frustrated by her colleagues' previous lack of cooperation and procrastination in making their donations, Cindy declined the responsibility. However, the company president, Lucille, begged. "But it's such a worthy cause. I can't believe you won't help out. If you don't help me, we won't reach our goal of 100 percent participation. And I'll look bad." Cindy caved in and agreed to do it, against her better judgment.

Cindy later complained, "Lucille made me feel so guilty, I had no choice. I didn't know how to get out of it."

In a different situation, Nadine hadn't seen her cousin Olga, who lived out of the country, for several years. Although Nadine tried to stay in contact, Olga returned her letters and calls infrequently. The week before Nadine was to attend a friend's wedding, Olga called to say she'd be in town for one day before leaving on a cruise and really wanted to see her cousin. Nadine explained she would be unavailable as she had a wedding to attend. Olga whined, "Oh, Nadine, I haven't seen you in so long. I really miss you. It really hurts me to think you won't make an effort to get together. After all, I'm coming all the way to Florida. My husband and I really want to see you."

Nadine, although she would have enjoyed seeing her cousin, didn't want to miss the wedding. She assertively replied, "Look, Olga, I love you and miss you, too. But don't try to make me feel guilty. I've had this commitment for several weeks. Please give me more notice the next time you plan on visiting. I will make seeing you my top priority."

The key to dealing with guilt-evoking confronters is to anticipate their resistance and be prepared to stick to your position. If Cindy had anticipated Lucille's guilt-evoking tactic, she could have been prepared to say (while simultaneously handing her a check), "Of course I want to help, but don't try to make me feel guilty. In fact, let me be the first person to contribute. However, I will not coordinate the drive this year. Please ask someone else for a change." Nadine, however, was prepared for her cousin's ploy. She refused to allow Olga to manipulate her through guilt. Nadine was faced with a tough personal decision. She decided what her choice was. Had she truly preferred to cancel her previous plans to accommodate Olga, that would have been fine. However, she would not allow her decision to be influenced by her cousin's intention to make her feel guilty. And she affectionately but assertively let Olga know.

### *"No, You've Got It All Wrong!"*

Some individuals will attempt to confront your assertiveness by skirting the real issue in order to throw you off track. They hope to make you unsure of yourself and your position. They will distort facts, bring up unrelated issues, or use faulty reasoning to confuse you into seeing things their way. You can expect to hear some variation of:

> You've got it all wrong.
> It doesn't work that way.
> What you're saying doesn't make sense.
> You misunderstood.

Kathleen's mother promised her the family heirloom piano on which she learned to play as a child. Kathleen's young niece, Kim, inadvertently let it slip that "Grandma" had promised *her* the piano for an upcoming birthday gift. Kathleen, hurt, approached her mother to clarify the situation and remind her of the promise made years before. Kathleen's mother attempted to justify her new promise to Kim by distorting the facts and making Kathleen feel guilty. "Oh, Kathleen, you misunderstood. I only promised you the piano thinking you would have children to enjoy it. Don't be so selfish. Don't you want little Kim to learn the piano?"

Fortunately, Kathleen wasn't buying into her mother's ploy to induce guilt or misrepresent information. She replied, "That's not the point, Mom. You promised me the piano before Kim was even born. You *never* implied that my having children was a condition for receiving it. If you're so concerned that she'll be deprived of a piano, buy her a new one! You just forgot your promise to me and you're trying to make me feel guilty for asking you to keep it." Kim's grandmother bought her a new piano and Kathleen felt great that she voiced her true feelings.

I observed the following conflict between two individuals while browsing in a boutique. A customer, Ms. Abbott, had just purchased $300 worth of new clothes at a shop where everything was reduced 40 percent the next day. It had always been the store's advertised policy that if any item was reduced within two weeks of purchase, the difference would be refunded to the customer.

Ms. Abbott returned the day of the sale to request the difference between what she had paid and the sale price. Mrs. Green, the manager, punched numbers into the computer, returned the $120 difference, and walked away to help another customer. Ms. Abbott called after her, "Excuse me. You've made an error. I'm still owed

$7.20." Mrs. Green was annoyed and snapped, "The computer doesn't make mistakes, that's what it says you get." Ms. Abbott patiently explained, "But you forgot to give me credit for the 6 percent sales tax already paid on the $300. I'm suppose to pay tax only on the actual amount of my purchase, which in this case is $180." The manager cut Ms. Abbott off, retorting, "That's what you get. You should be grateful you got what you did. I didn't have to give you anything back. Do you presume to be smarter than the computer?"

Ms. Abbott wasn't going to be thrown off track by the manager's bluster, illogic, and attempts to confuse the situation. As her polite explanation was ignored, she decided to escalate her response. She assertively replied, "Number one: Please don't act as though you are doing me any favors. This shop has an advertised policy of refunding the actual price paid within two weeks of purchase. Number two: The computer is only as good as the person using it. You never programmed it to calculate the 6 percent sales tax on the $120 refund which is also due me. For your information, the amount if $7.20." Mrs. Green finally refunded the difference.

Later, noticing Ms. Abbott in the parking lot of the shopping center, I couldn't resist complimenting her, "I really admire the way you handled the situation at the boutique. You stuck to your guns and didn't let that manager take advantage of you." She thanked me for the support and confessed, "I almost left without the $7.20 tax refund thinking it wasn't worth it. But I would have hated myself later had I left just to avoid the hassle."

Dealing with a toxic person who wants to throw you off balance by making you unsure of yourself can be extremely frustrating and unpleasant. An irrational person's goal is to sidetrack you in order to make you doubt your own sanity or ability to reason logically. When you're sure of your position, keep repeating it. Do not deviate from it. Have the courage to challenge this type of confronter in an assertive, no-nonsense, hostility-free fashion. Make your expectations crystal clear in a calm, polite manner, as did Kathleen and Ms. Abbott. And, don't hesitate to "escalate" your responses if necessary. When the illogical confronter sees you have the strength of your convictions, you are likely to prevail.

### *"You're Too Sensitive!"*

There are confronters who will use your assertiveness as an excuse to criticize you further. They are stunned that you have rallied against their inappropriate remarks. In an effort to save face and justify their behavior, they criticize you for some shortcoming. By making you feel worse, they make themselves feel better. These criticizing confronters try to project their faults onto you. You've probably heard such criticisms as:

> You're too sensitive.
> Don't be so emotional.
> You have no sense of humor.
> You're selfish.
> You always overreact.
> I wasn't insulting you; don't be so paranoid.

After her divorce, Fern preferred to spend evenings and weekends reading and watching television. She had no interest in meeting new people. Tammy invited Fern to a dinner party to meet Tammy's recently divorced brother. During the course of the evening, Tammy laughingly announced, "Poor Fern! She doesn't have much of a social life. We had to get her a date!" Fern assertively replied, "Thanks for the concern but I really can get my own dates. Maybe I haven't wanted much of a social life." Tammy retorted, "I didn't mean anything by that. You're too sensitive."

Fern chose not to dignify the remark. She appeared unruffled by Tammy's criticism and continued the previous conversation as if it had never been interrupted.

Karen was a particularly creative graphic artist at an advertising agency. John, a coworker, frequently made cracks about her inability to operate electronic devices or do anything mechanical. "She doesn't even know which end of a screwdriver to use," "I'm surprised she can draw a straight line," and "It's a good thing she can draw because she can't figure out how to use a camera" were typical examples. The remarks bothered Karen, but she had always ignored them.

Two weeks after hearing me speak about assertive communication, Karen called to say how proud she was for finally asserting herself with John. She was unable to open a stubborn lock on a supply cabinet. John opened it, smirking, "You probably need someone to show you where to put your car key in the ignition."

Karen defended herself. "John, your wisecracks are insulting. Please stop making them." Instead of apologizing, John confronted her. "I was only joking. You have no sense of humor." Karen felt it was time to escalate her response. She calmly said, "I suggest you use a dictionary to learn the difference between jokes and insults. As I requested earlier, please refrain from making those hurtful wisecracks."

Depending on your personality and personal style, you might decide to ignore the criticizing confronter or return the challenge. Fern chose to disregard Tammy's criticism. It was clear to all present at the dinner party that Fern handled herself assertively and confidently. Karen, on the other hand, had suffered John's verbal abuse for months. She was determined to no longer listen passively while John made her the butt of his jokes. Karen first tried a polite, mild assertion. When it didn't work, she decided to change her strategy. Karen's last retort to John's criticism of her justified assertion was strong and she knew it. However, she chose to respond this way. An assertion such as, "I disagree John. I have an excellent sense of humor," would have been fine, too. Karen should be applauded for summoning the will to say what she wanted to say for a long time. As long as she was pleased with her choice, it was the right one for her. Experiment with a variety of styles to see which ones fit you best. Respond any way you like!

Women become especially insecure when their assertiveness is attacked by the criticizing confronter. You might be hesitant to risk facing criticism because your self-esteem and confidence is often based on what others think of you. It's this fear of criticism that makes you most vulnerable to verbal attacks. Being criticized may cause you to doubt the benefits of assertive communication. Well, don't doubt them for a second. Criticizing confronters want to put you on the defensive to control and even to intimidate you. Usually, they are jealous or insecure themselves and want to portray you as the one with the faults. Simply refuse to accept the confronters' critical projections onto you.

There are a couple of pitfalls to avoid when dealing with criticizing confronters. Avoid becoming defensive. Refrain from attempting to convince them that their assessment of you is incorrect. They don't necessarily believe you are really "selfish," "paranoid," "humorless," or "too sensitive," and so forth. They are trying to push your buttons and put you on the defensive. Don't let them. Four additional techniques for dealing with these abusers include: 1. Simply Disagree With Them, 2. State Your Position, 3. Pleasantly Agree With Them, and 4. The Broken Record Technique, which is described with examples below.

*Example:* You are planning to relax at home after a hectic day at work. Your daughter knows how tired you are but accuses you of being selfish for refusing to chauffeur her to the mall to meet her friends. Simply disagree: "I don't agree with your point of view," or "I disagree, I'm very giving." If she persists, you might state your position: "No, I'm generous. It's selfish of you to constantly expect me to be at your beck and call."

*Example:* Your husband refers to you as "thunder thighs." He tells you that you're "too sensitive" when you tell him the expression bothers you. You might say, "I disagree, I'm really quite thick-skinned. I simply find the remark insulting." You might state your position: "No, I'm not too sensitive. It's insensitive to call me that!" Or, you might agree with him: "You're right, I'm sensitive. So please stop calling me that."

*Example:* A colleague says you have no sense of humor when you object to her inappropriate jokes. Respond: "I disagree completely. I have a great sense of humor," and walk away. You could state your position: "You're the one with no sense of humor. Your jokes aren't even funny. Do not subject me to them again!" Or, you might agree with her: "You're right. So why not save your jokes for someone who can appreciate them!"

## *"Why Are You Picking on Me?"*

Some verbal abusers have had their own way for a long time. They may react to your assertion by looking insulted or saying you don't like them. When caught at their "put-down" game, they love to protest their innocence and play the victim. When you assert yourself with these individuals, they'll feign innocence and confront you by acting as though you have victimized them. Be prepared to hear:

> I didn't do anything.
> Why are you picking on me?
> I don't deserve that.
> What did I do?
> I didn't mean anything bad.
> All I said was...

Elizabeth surprised her sister Erin with a new computer for her birthday. She had it all set up and ready to go when Erin came home from law school on spring break. Excited, Erin couldn't wait to try it out. But Erin was extremely disappointed when the printer wouldn't work, and she went about checking all the connections. She found the printer cable was not connected to the proper computer port. Her voice was dripping with sarcasm as she said, "That was really smart, Elizabeth." Elizabeth asserted herself. "That was uncalled for. Here I'm knocking myself out to do something nice for you. All you do is criticize me." Erin pretended to appear insulted, "Hey, I didn't say anything wrong. I said that was really smart. I paid you a compliment." "Oh Erin," Elizabeth sighed, "your 'poor me' act doesn't fool anyone." Erin apologized for her remark and thanked Elizabeth for being such a great sister. Together they got the system working perfectly.

There are two good ways to handle "victims" when they react to your appropriate assertiveness in that phony "injured" way. 1. Ignore them. You've made your point. They know they're not fooling anyone. 2. Directly confront them. Be sure to do it in a hostility-free manner.

On many occasions, I've said with a grin and a twinkle in my eye,

"Cut the nonsense, Joe. Don't play the victim with me. You know perfectly well your remarks were out of line." In my experience, the victim routine is then abandoned and the episode ends gracefully.

### The Broken Record Technique

As you've seen, your assertive communication will keep would-be confronters very busy! They may try to confuse you, criticize you for refusing their requests or complaining about their behavior, or attempt to manipulate you through guilt. They will persist until they wear you down and you agree to accommodate them.

The Broken Record Technique is a great way to deal with confronters who refuse to accept your valid assertions. It provides you with yet another option for dealing with these difficult people. All .you have to do is give the same response to each of the confronter's comebacks. Simply repeat the same words over and over, like a broken record. No matter how persistent critics or manipulators are, the broken record strategy will cause them to give up. After all, arguing with a broken record is impossible!

*Example:* I gave my college class five weeks to complete an assignment. I made it very clear that no late papers would be accepted for any reason. Several students approached me on the due date without their work. Here's how one student attempted to manipulate me into granting an exception.

Dan: I'm really sorry Dr. Dale, but I had an emergency and couldn't complete my paper.
Me: Sorry, Dan. You had five weeks' notice. I'm not accepting any late papers.
Dan: But my computer printer wouldn't work last night.
Me: That's unfortunate, Dan, but you had five weeks' notice. I'm not accepting any late papers.
Dan: I have it right here on my floppy disk.
Me: I'm sure you do, but you had five weeks' notice. I'm not accepting any late papers.
Dan: Oh, come on, Dr. Dale. If I don't get at least a B in your

class, my grade point average will drop.

Me: It happens, Dan, but you had five weeks' notice. I'm not accepting any late papers.

Dan: I might lose my scholarship.

Me: That would be terrible, but you had five weeks' notice, I'm not accepting any late papers.

Dan: You are being very unfair, Dr. Dale.

Me: I'm sure you feel it's unfair, Dan, but you had five weeks' notice. I'm not accepting any late papers.

*Example:* Remember Cindy, the insurance agent, who was angry with herself for agreeing to coordinate her company's United Way campaign for the fifth consecutive year? She could have used the Broken Record Technique with Lucille.

Lucille: Cindy, you'll coordinate the annual United Way campaign this year, won't you?

Cindy: No, I have too many commitments already. Please ask someone else for a change.

Lucille: But it's such a worthy cause. I can't believe you won't help.

Cindy: No Lucille. I have too many other commitments. Please ask someone else.

Lucille: If you don't help me, we won't reach our goal of 100 percent participation.

Cindy: No, I'm over-committed right now. We have lots of capable employees. Please ask someone else for a change.

Lucille: But I was really counting on you Cindy.

Cindy: Lucille, I will not accept a guilt grip. I will not coordinate the drive this year. Please ask someone else for a change.

The beauty of the Broken Record Technique is that it is successful with most confronters. Observe how Barbara uses it in response to the various ploys Steve attempts with her.

Steve: But I like calling you "Barbie."

Barbara: As I've mentioned before, I don't care for that nickname. Please call me by my name, Barbara.

Steve: (Using aggression) You must have had a fight with your
   husband last night.
Barbara: My husband has nothing to do with this. Please call
   me by my name, Barbara.
Steve: (Playing the victim) Don't be so hard on me. I don't
   think you like me.
Barbara: Please don't play the injured party. I simply want you
   to call me by my name, Barbara.
Steve: (Trying to divert the issue) My sister's name is Barbara.
   She loves to be called "Barbie."
Barbara: By all means, call your sister Barbie. But, please call
   *me* by my name, Barbara.
Steve: (Using criticism) You really are sensitive, aren't you?
Barbara: Whether I am or not is not the point. Please call me
   Barbara.

As you can see, the Broken Record Technique works well in many
situations. Use it to discourage persistent confronters or manipulators. They will quickly learn that you mean what you say!

**EXERCISE**

Describe three situations in which your efforts to be assertive were
met with some form of confrontation. Explain how you handled
your confronters. Would you handle them differently if they
confronted you in the same way on another occasion?

*Example:* Bradley and June were dancing at their wedding
reception, enjoying their special day. When the music stopped,
June's aunt and uncle asked the newlyweds for a ride to the airport.
They had to leave the reception early to make their flight home.
Bradley explained that he didn't want to leave his guests and
offered to call June's relatives a cab. June's aunt whined, "But kids,
we love you so much. We came all this way to see you. Taking us to
the airport will give us a chance to spend some time together. It
won't take very long. You'll be back at your party in no time."
Sighing, Bradley and June agreed to drive them to the airport.
   Bradley told me that if he had to do it all over again, he would

have absolutely refused to be manipulated. He wished he had said, "No, Aunt Irene, we don't want to leave our other guests. We do love you very much and hope to visit you soon. As I said, I'll be happy to call you a cab." He would have used the Broken Record Technique and repeated his position as many times as necessary until his relatives dropped their unreasonable request. To use his words, "I'll never allow June's aunt, or anyone else for that matter, to lay a guilt trip on me again!"

## It Was Nice Knowing You

Some users and verbal abusers may not confront you. They may reject you completely for your assertiveness. Some may confront you, then reject you! After all, you no longer serve their purpose. You're no longer their submissive doormat. If acquaintances or so-called friends no longer want to associate with you, accept their decision. You must realize that they weren't worth your time and effort to begin with. They never treated you with the dignity and respect you deserve. In fact, they did all they could to undermine your self-esteem.

Of course, many individuals with whom you've appropriately asserted yourself will not confront you at all. They might offer a sincere apology for the behavior which triggered your assertion in the first place. You may be pleasantly surprised to find that they treat you with newfound respect and admiration. As mentioned in the previous chapter, your direct honest communication may be the catalyst that starts them on the road to reform. If it doesn't, you should reject the users and abusers. Let them go. In *Toxic People,* communications consultant Lillian Glass, Ph.D., describes her "Unplug Technique." She counsels, "Visualize yourself unplugging from them, as if from an electric socket. You need to become devoid of emotion regarding them. Just let them out of your life for good and never look back."

Letting them go doesn't mean that you're trying to harm them. You're simply trying to help yourself. So, feel good. Feel good because you know you have taken the steps necessary to move forward with your life and to feel good about yourself.

# 4

# *Just Say "No"*

At an elegant luncheon banquet to raise scholarship money for our college, I was seated with five women of much higher administrative status than I. The beautiful floral centerpieces which adorned the tables were to be raffled off to one guest at each table. Pilar, a vice president, had her heart set on winning the centerpiece from our table. She was clearly disappointed when another individual's number was selected. As the banquet was drawing to a close, she noticed an unclaimed centerpiece on an already vacated table. Pilar desperately wanted it, but she was too embarrassed to claim it herself. She turned to me ("low man on the totem pole" in the administrative hierarchy), and sweetly asked, "Paulette, would you please carry that floral arrangement out for me?"

All eyes were on me awaiting my response. (By the way, there was nothing wrong with Pilar's arm. She simply wanted me to do her dirty work.) I rapidly considered alternatives and possible excuses. I knew excuses would sound feeble. Pilar was not interested in them anyhow. Knowing that I would hate myself for agreeing to be her lackey, I swallowed hard and politely replied, "No Pilar, I'd rather not." Stunned by my refusal, Pilar commented to the group that I was being uncooperative. Her remark was met by silence from all present. She actually retrieved the centerpiece and carried it out herself.

I have a confession to make. My first reaction was to carry the flowers just to appear cooperative. However, I would have despised myself for being submissive. Today, almost fifteen years later, I still feel good about the way I handled the episode.

We have all experienced situations in which we feel obligated to say "yes," even when our gut reaction is to say "no." Why is this? Why do we find ourselves giving in when we clearly don't want to? Most women have an extremely tough time saying "no" for one or more reasons.

Many women believe it's their responsibility to meet everyone's needs. We continually put ourselves last by running errands, doing favors, and generally accommodating others when it is personally inconvenient to do so. We are taught from an early age to be responsive and acquiescent. As wives and mothers, we frequently feel it is selfish to put ourselves first and regularly defer to the needs and desires of friends and family members. This occurs at great personal expense. We begin to feel used for constantly allowing others to take advantage of us. Our self-esteem and self-respect fly out the window as a result of our efforts to be perennial people-pleasers.

In *Real Moments,* author Barbara DeAngelis, Ph.D., writes, "The problem is that when we make pleasing others a priority, we often do it at the price of neglecting to please ourselves. Be being so self-sacrificing, we deprive ourselves of the time and opportunity we seek. We become disconnected from the core of who we are."

Some women are concerned with earning the acceptance and approval of everyone with everything they do or say. They don't want to be unpopular or disliked by appearing to be disagreeable. They believe that saying "no" decreases their chances of approval and acceptance by all. Unfortunately, your self-respect suffers when you become more concerned with what others think of you rather than how you feel about yourself.

The vast majority of women interviewed want to avoid conflicts at all costs. They hesitate to say no for fear of triggering an argument with someone who is adamant about getting his own way. They simply acquiesce to keep the peace. They believe submissiveness to be the path of least resistance at the moment. However, the path of least resistance may not be the best route to take. Even Oprah Winfrey had admitted that she'd rather run out and get hit by a truck than trigger a conflict with someone who has taken advantage of her. If you end up feeling used or annoyed with yourself for suppressing your needs, then saying "yes" is not in your best interest. The loss of self-respect you suffer is much more detrimental than the brief confrontation sparked by a difficult individual.

Saying "yes" to avoid a conflict is generally the preferred course of action in certain situations. Say "yes" if the matter at hand is not at all important to you or if you truly feel, "Oh well, it's six of one, half dozen of another." After all, there is a great pleasure in being accommodating when possible. However, this does not mean that you must allow users and abusers to take advantage of your good nature. They have no right to expect you to adjust to their inclinations upon demand.

The people in your life will always make demands on your time. If you don't say "no" when you want to, you are not in control of your own life. It's time you begin saying "no" when you really feel like it!

### Explanations Versus Excuses

Offering a brief explanation to let the other person know the reason behind your refusal may help you feel better about delivering a "no" message. However, a firm direct "no" followed by a brief honest explanation is not the same as a "no" justified by an invented excuse.

Your "no" accompanied by a truthful comment shows that your decision is your preference. It assertively demonstrates you are willing to take responsibility for your refusal. "No, I won't loan you any more money. You still haven't paid back what you owe me" or "Sorry, I'm unable to loan you money. I'm not in a position to make any loans at this time," are examples of firm direct *no*'s followed by brief honest explanations. (Chapter 9, "Speak Up on the Job," elaborates on the advantages of providing a brief, honest explanation when saying "no" in typical workplace situations.)

Even though you decline a request, expressing appreciation for having been asked may be appropriate in certain situations. It's another technique that will help you feel better about saying "no." "Thanks for thinking of me, but I won't serve on the committee this year. I have too many other commitments" or "I don't care to contribute, but thank your for calling me," are examples.

An invented excuse shows you are a victim of circumstance. It pretends to blame a situation beyond your control for refusal. "Sorry, I can't loan you the money. I forgot my wallet this morning" or "I can't serve on the committee this year. I have to drive my son to soccer practice every afternoon," are examples of invented excuses.

Excuses might offer you a quick escape from assertively refusing a request. However, they frequently end up causing you more stress and anxiety than saying "no" to begin with.

Karina found it extremely difficult to refuse unwanted dates or invitations. She committed herself to everyone and everything knowing full well she intended to break the commitment with an excuse. She always called to cancel at the last minute, saying, "I'm not feeling well," "I have to go out of town unexpectedly," or "My mother is sick, I have to stay with her," and so on. She then became a prisoner in her own home. She was afraid to go out for fear someone she knew would see her and catch her in the lie. Karina finally learned to say no, up front, to invitations she didn't want to accept and to affably thank the individual for thinking of her. She happily finds herself with less stress and more time to do the things she *wants* to do.

### Decide: Yes or No

Ask yourself, *Do I really want to say no? Am I saying yes only to avoid a conflict? Will I be annoyed with myself later on for giving in? Will I feel resentful that my time has been infringed upon?* If you can answer yes to any of these questions, then you should say *no!*

Consider both sides of the situation so that you can make a decision that is in your best interest. Of course you should say yes if you truly want to. Why not? Most women enjoy being gracious and delight in giving generously of their time and energy to appreciative individuals. They will happily inconvenience themselves and perform favors in the name of friendship and love. It's wonderful to be supportive of friends, relatives, colleagues, and children.

Decide how you prefer to respond. Say yes if you want to say yes. If you'd like, qualify your "yes" with conditions. It's perfectly okay to say, "Yes, but…" or "Yes, if.…" Chapter 5, "Buy Time Before Responding," elaborates on this technique. Just don't say "yes" when you want to say "no!" There are many styles and techniques that may be used to deliver effective "no" messages. Experiment with a variety of responses. Depending upon your personality, you will favor some over others. Choose those with which you will be most comfortable.

### The Assertive No

Once you've decided to refuse an offer or decline a request, you need to make your position clear. The following examples will help you compare the most common ways of delivering "no" messages.

*Situation:* A friend asks you to feed and walk her dog several times a day while she is on vacation.

An *unassertive* way to refuse is to invent an excuse to avoid consenting to the request. An unassertive "no" message might be, "I'd really love to take care of your dog but I'm going out of town myself for a few days." Fibs might serve your purpose on occasion. However, you run the embarrassing risk of being caught in your lie at a later time.

An *aggressive* way to refuse is to verbally attack the individual for asking you in the first place. An aggressive "no" message might be, "Are you too cheap to hire a professional pet caretaker? I have more important things to do than babysit your dog." The aggressive response will certainly make your point. However, it will probably do irreparable damage to your friendship or relationship. It is certainly possible to reject a request without being insulting or embarrassing

An *assertive* way to refuse is simply to say "no." An assertive "no" message might be, "No, I won't be able to help you out next week. I have too many prior commitments." It's appropriate to offer a brief explanation for your refusal, but it's certainly not required. That's your decision depending upon how you feel at the time. A clear, "No, I won't be able to, but thanks for thinking of me," will do the trick politely and assertively.

*Situation:* A friend asks if you have time to talk. She wants to maliciously gossip about Leah, a mutual friend.

An *unassertive* "no" message might be, "I really don't have time to talk right now. I promised my sister I'd drive her to the doctor. I don't want her to be late for the appointment."

An *aggressive* "no" message might be, "Don't you have anything better to do in your free time? You are always bad-mouthing others. I wonder what you say about me behind my back."

An *assertive* "no" message might be, "I would love to spend some time with you, but I'd prefer not to discuss Leah or her problems. Let's have some coffee while you tell me what you've been up to."

### EXERCISE

Now you try it. Formulate *unassertive, aggressive,* and *assertive* "no" messages to the following requests.

*Situation:* A coworker invites you to a party. You have no specific reasons for refusing other than you'd prefer to relax at home alone.

Deliver an unassertive "no" message:

Deliver an aggressive "no" message:

Deliver an assertive "no" message:

*Situation:* Your dinner companion invites you to join him in having cocktails before dinner. You politely declined once, but he continues to urge you to have a drink.

Deliver an unassertive "no" message:

Deliver an aggressive "no" message:

Deliver an assertive "no" message:

*Situation:* A friend asks to borrow your car while you are out of town for the weekend.

Deliver an unassertive "no" message:

Deliver an aggressive "no" message

Deliver an assertive "no" message:

*Situation:* Your cousin asks you to cosign a bank loan for her new mortgage.

Deliver an unassertive "no" message:

Deliver an aggressive "no" message:

Deliver an assertive "no" message:

*Situation:* An acquaintance asks to borrow money promising to repay it the following week. She is notorious for forgetting to repay her obligations.

Deliver an unassertive "no" message:

Deliver an aggressive "no" message:

Deliver an assertive "no" message:

*Situation:* A stranger asks you to help carry her luggage out to a waiting cab at the airport.

Deliver an unassertive "no" message:

Deliver an aggressive "no" message:

Deliver an assertive "no" message:

## Be Direct and Firm

I refused to yield to an arrogant stranger during a recent business trip. Having boarded my flight early, I was comfortably seated in the aisle seat to which I was assigned. "You're in my seat," a not-so-gentlemanly gentleman abruptly announced. "I beg your pardon," I politely replied pointing to the seat assignment on my boarding pass, proving I was in the right place. He displayed his ticket stub showing the same seat designation. "I guess we were both inadvertently assigned to the same seat. The center seat in this row is available," I pleasantly indicated. Hands on hips, he barked, "I prefer the aisle, please move." Looking him straight in the eyes, I replied, "No, I too, prefer the aisle. Let's abide by the first-come-first-served principle!" (Translation: I'm not moving!) Realizing that he would simple have to take "no" for an answer, he stormed away in a huff searching for an unoccupied seat.

Some of you might be thinking, Gee, I wish I could react quickly, I can never think of what to say on the spur of the moment. Don't be concerned about your ability to think up a lot to say at a moment's notice. A simple no or "I'm not moving, I got here first," would have worked just fine in this situation.

Sure, I could have avoided this mildly unpleasant conflict by immediately yielding to the passenger's request and changing my seat. And I would have, too, if sitting in an aisle seat didn't happen to be a strong personal preference. But saying yes simply to appear agreeable or to avoid the conflict would have left me irked with myself for not being assertive. Remember, the way you feel about yourself over the long haul is more important than how some user or abuser feels about you for the moment.

My aunt frequently complains that a neighbor refuses to take "no" for an answer whenever the neighbor wants something. In reality, a remark like that says more about my aunt than her neighbor. A person who won't take "no" for an answer is generally dealing with someone who doesn't say "no" with conviction.

Saying "no" directly is simple and effective. It's a courageous, honest choice that can be executed politely and firmly. Be sure to speak decisively using a downward intonation. If you respond too softly or tentatively, you will appear unsure and hesitant. You will be open to manipulation, as is my aunt. Those who would take advantage of you will apply more pressure to get you to give in.

Keep in mind that just because certain individuals are not pleased about something doesn't mean it shouldn't happen or exist. It's not their inalienable right to please themselves at your expense. It's not your fault they're not happy. Nor is it your responsibility to inconvenience yourself to manipulate their environment to content them. Don't hesitate to allow your own preferences to take precedence for a change. Remember, I'm not talking about refusing to say "yes" to someone who genuinely needs your help. I'm talking about saying "no" to selfish or manipulative requests. This holds true even if the "user" happens to be someone in an authority position or someone famous. Refuse to be intimidated by someone of so-called fame or importance.

An internationally known Pulitzer Prize–winning journalist had been the keynote speaker at our college's Arts and Letters Day celebration. After his address, Cara, a member of our faculty, chauffeured him back to Miami International Airport for his return flight. He had an air of arrogant superiority and acted annoyed at Cara's efforts to engage him in friendly conversation. Before getting out, he asked if he could throw his dirty Styrofoam coffee cup on the floor of her car. Flabbergasted by the request, Cara responded, "That's fine." She really wanted to say, "No, I prefer you didn't. Please find a trash receptacle for your garbage." Cara explained she didn't have the nerve to respond with her gut reaction. She didn't want to displease the college's esteemed guest. However, she still wishes to this day that she had had the courage to say what she really felt.

Had the celebrated writer been pleasant and affable, Cara would have been delighted to dispose of his cup for him. However, she resented his rude, condescending manner and later regretted her failure to assert her preference.

I was gratified when Gail, a participant in one of my workshops, emphatically asserted her position when invited by her married supervisor to begin a discreet affair. Instead of becoming outraged and screaming "sexual harassment," she retorted quietly but firmly,

"No, do not come on to me again and I will forget this ever happened. I have no intention of becoming anyone's clandestine diversion." (The supervisor never bothered her again and treated her with respect until his transfer a year later.) Gail's choice of words was certainly articulate and effective. However, as mentioned earlier, a firm "No, not interested" would have served the purpose.

I was twenty-four years old and had just started as a full-time college instructor. A prominent administrator caught me unaware in an empty corridor. He put his arms around me, saying "You'd like me to kiss you, wouldn't you?" Fuming, I broke away, "No, there is nothing I would like less. I suggest you *never* approach me again." He never did. Many less-assertive female employees weren't so fortunate. His shenanigans went on for years until he was formally charged with sexual harassment and found guilty by the state ethics commission.

Psychologists recommend you begin your response with the word "no," otherwise, you are likely to end up responding "maybe" or "yes."

Saying "no" takes many possible forms:

No, thanks—I'm not interested.
No, I don't want to.
No, that's not convenient.
No, I won't.
No, I don't care to discuss it.
No, I can't make it but thanks for the invitation.
No, I disagree, please make another recommendation.
No, I'll pass.

Simply shake your head and maintain direct eye contact.

Some women feel better about using humor, tongue-in-cheek wit, cheerful evasion, or even a long hard stare with raised eyebrows to convey "no." Responding in this manner can be a humorous and effective way to make your position clear. It can lighten the atmosphere and show that you harbor no ill will. For example, when the famous journalist asked if he could throw the dirty cup in Cara's car, she could have cheerfully replied, "Is there a shortage of trash cans around here?," "I'm sure there are handy garbage bins inside," "I know my car isn't showroom new, but I didn't think it resembled a garbage bag!" or even, "I bet you wouldn't ask me that if my car was a Ferrari!"

### Don't Feel Forced to Tell All

Women frequently feel compelled to provide all kinds of information just because it's requested of them. Ellen Alderman and Caroline Kennedy in their book *The Right to Privacy* point out how a surprising amount of information requested of us is actually voluntary. Although we might prefer to keep it confidential, we submit and provide it as if it were mandatory.

It's very important to remember that you have the right to privacy and the right to say "no." My accountant, Donna, a frequent customer in computer and electronics stores, complained about the common practice of asking shoppers for their names, addresses, and phone numbers when making a purchase. When I asked her why she didn't just refuse the request, she replied, "I didn't know I could." I said, "Donna, if you don't want to disclose personal information, you don't have to. They'll still be happy to take your money!" Several weeks later, she proudly reported that when she verbally asserted herself by saying, "No, I don't want to be in your computer, just let me pay for my purchase," the clerk simply shrugged and mumbled, "Fine with me." Donna didn't realize how easy it was to say "no" and still feel good about herself.

We also have the right to say no when someone asks an intimate or personal question. Never feel obligated to tell a nosy meddler what he or she wants to hear. Your response should please yourself. You must first decide what or how much you want to divulge. For example, if someone asks you your weight or why you don't have children, you have the right to answer any way you want. If you want to tell all, fine. That's your choice. But it's also your choice to refuse to answer.

Humor and cheerful evasion work particularly well when personal or even intimate information is being sought. For example, when asked your salary or your age, the evasive humorous classics "Not enough" and "Over twenty-one" are good choices. If ever asked how many lovers you've had, the retorts, "Nosy, aren't we?" or "More than one, less than a million" always reveal that you don't choose to divulge the news to the nosy busybody!

Try developing some playful responses of your own. When I'm asked an inappropriate personal question, I like to flash my best enigmatic "Mona Lisa" smile and say, "I'd prefer not to say," or "I'll take the Fifth on that question!"

Answering an inappropriate question with a question of your own may be the way to go in some situations. In a letter to Ann Landers, a woman in Denver describes how this tact can be used successfully in response to inappropriate personal inquiries. She wrote:

Dear Ann,

I am writing in response to the letter from the mother of triplets and a six-month-old who was sick and tired of rude questions from strangers.

If a woman has no children, she hears, "When are you having kids? Why aren't you having any?" If a woman has one child, she hears, "When are you going to have another? You don't want your baby to be lonely, do you?"

If a woman has several children close in age, she gets crude remarks about her active sex life or her husband's hormonal output.

People who are asked personal questions by insensitive clods need never feel obligated to respond. Your long ago line, "Why would *you* be interested in *that?*" is the perfect rejoinder!

Of course, your playful response, cheerful evasion, or rhetorical question, "Why would you be interested in that?" might not do the trick. There are plenty of insensitive clods who just won't take a hint. You may need to escalate your response in order to get through to these people. As the following anecdotes show, stating your position firmly and directly may be the only way to make it clear to some people that you don't care to provide the information they are seeking.

When I was nineteen years old, I had a summer job as a receptionist for a well-known director of TV commercials at the film company's production studio on Park Avenue. This director frequently asked his female employees about their personal lives. Looking to enliven a rainy and otherwise dull afternoon with some juicy conversation, he called to me across the room. "Paulette, tell us about your sex life. Are you still a virgin?"

Flabbergasted, I muttered, "Oh, I'll take the Fifth on that!" "In this office, no one takes the Fifth when *I* ask a question," the director quipped before asking me again. This time I escalated my response by stating my position, "I prefer not to answer such a personal question." To my horror, he persisted. He was clearly hell-bent on getting me to respond. I had no choice but to escalate my response further. Swallowing hard, I directly met his gaze and replied, "That's none of your business. Please don't ask me again." I fully expected to be shown the door. Instead, the director simply glared at me for a moment and wordlessly left the room. He pretty much ignored me until I went back to college in the fall

My mother's friend, Laura, is a lifelong people pleaser in her late sixties. She lives in government-subsidized housing for the elderly. Laura dislikes when acquaintances ask her how much rent she personally contributes. Usually, she feels obligated to respond truthfully and completely to all inquiries even though she'd rather not. Recently, when asked about her housing costs by her nosy friend, Minnie, Laura pleasantly replied, with a question of her own, "Why do you want to know that?" "Just curious," Minnie laughed, and repeated her original question. This time, Laura escalated her response and politely stated in no uncertain terms, "Minnie, my rent is really my business. I'd prefer not to discuss it." Laura reported feeling marvelously empowered at finally being able to say what she wanted to say and not what she thought was expected of her. As you can see, the ability to say "no" doesn't automatically come with age and maturity. It needs to be learned. With practice, it can be acquired at any age. As in Laura's case, it's never too late to feel better about yourself.

## Say No Without Explaining

Many of us feel an overwhelming need to justify our responses with a plethora of reasons or lengthy explanations. For some reason, we cling to the hope that our sincere, rational, and candid explanations are going to have an impact on the other person's way of thinking. We've all been targeted by representatives of charities seeking donations. They know how and where to find us. They contact us at work, at home, and by fax. I've even been called on my cellular phone while riding in the car! Saying "You caught me at a bad time" serves no worthwhile purpose. They will hound you until a "good" time is found.

Maria, a dear friend, never says "no." She always ends up pledging ten or fifteen dollars when she doesn't even like the particular charity. She described her typical response to a request for a contribution.

"Oh this is really a bad time for me to make a pledge. We have lots of expenses right now. Our roof is leaking and the car insurance is due, etc., etc." "Of course," she continued her description to me, "they persist. So I finally cave in and commit to a donation I don't want to make."

I told her, "Maria, this song-and-dance routine about personal financial problems has got to stop. These solicitors don't care about your leaking roof or car insurance premiums. They're trained to persevere until you agree to send a check. So, stop apologizing and making excuses. Say, "No, I don't care to contribute." I even suggested that she add, "Thanks for calling me, but please don't contact me again regarding this."

We frequently find ourselves with no time to do the things we want to do because of our desire for universal acceptance. Dr. Shannon Brumfield, in *Fix It Before It Breaks,* describes valuable advice given to Althea, a busy mother, who is repeatedly asked to participate in school, church, and community volunteer activities. After listening to Althea complain that she is besieged by organizations asking for her help on special projects, her friend Susan commented that Althea had no time for herself. She suggested Althea not accept any more volunteer jobs. Althea decided to explain exactly why her time is valuable to the next person requesting her help. Susan aptly counseled, "They are not interested in a detailed explanation of your needs, hopes, dreams, and goals! Take Nancy Reagan's advise and 'just say no,' sweetly but firmly."

The scenarios may be different: being asked to make a donation, buy a product or service, babysit for a friend's wild children, care for a vacationing neighbor's pets, or any number of other favors that may be inconvenient for you at the time. But one thing never changes. People who don't want to take no for an answer rarely want to listen to your excuses or see your point of view. They have their own agenda and intend to hang on to it. Don't waste your breath, time, or energy. Thank them for thinking of you, if you need to, then just say no!

### Don't Be Intimidated by Experts

Many women are particularly reluctant to exercise their option to say "no" when dealing with experts, especially doctors. They are so brainwashed into believing they must blindly follow their physi-cian's advice without protesting, questioning, or disagreeing, even when common sense dictates otherwise. They may do this out of respect for authority, a desire to please, or a fear of offending the doctor. I used to be extremely reluctant to speak up with my doctors. After all, who was I? What did I know?

After reading *Examining Your Doctor,* by Timothy B. McCall, M.D., I learned that assertive patients get better care. Dr. McCall summarizes a study done at the New England Medical Center in Boston. Researchers trained a group of patients to take control of the physician–patient relationship by asking and expressing their feelings. They discovered that the assertive patients stayed healthier than similar patients who never learned to be assertive.

Well, after being unnecessarily inconvenienced by some of my doctor's recommendations, I realized it was time to speak up. I recognized that physicians, like the rest of us, were fallible.

*Example:* After setting my four-year-old son's broken arm, the orthopedic surgeon advised it be X-rayed on a weekly basis. This seemed excessive to me. If so many X-rays were not absolutely necessary, I did not want to subject my preschooler to them. Rather than just accept the recommendation, I told the doctor I didn't agree and asked him to please explain why so many X-rays were required. He immediately saw the validity to my concern and changed his recommendation to include a schedule of fewer X-rays over the six-week healing period.

*Example:* My doctor prescribed an antibiotic for a throat infection. I mentioned that this particular medication had previously caused me unpleasant side effects. He immediately discounted my lament and informed me the discomfort had to be due to other factors, as this particular drug wouldn't have the effects I described. I disagreed with this position, and asked him to prescribe a different antibiotic. He did; I felt great in a couple of days.

Dr. McCall advises that we should only agree to a treatment or particular course of action when we feel it's right for us, not because our doctor favors it over others. He suggests that a nonthreatening way to assert your preference might be to tell the specialist you're undecided and will get back to him with a decision. This is certainly the best course of action when you need to make a decision about major surgery or a treatment plan likely to significantly affect your quality of life.

Never feel pressured into immediately agreeing with a recommendation just because it's coming from an "expert." Have the confidence to trust your own judgment and know what's right for you.

### Don't Feel Obligated Just Because It's Family

Saying "no" in one or another of it's forms to friends or family is often problematic. However, to preserve your mental health and sanity, you must rise to the occasion when warranted. Most people I know who live in Florida, as I do, are often faced with the dilemma of dealing with unwanted and self-invited house guests. We frequently find our mouths saying "Sure, I'd love you to stay with me" when our guts are screaming, "No, no, please stay in a hotel!"

Year after year, we say to ourselves, "Never again. Next year I'm going to tell them how I feel." But, we don't. That great lady, Ann Landers, is a firm believer in assertive communication. The following column appeared in the *Miami Herald* (March 15, 1996). Ann's advice, as always, is priceless.

Dear Ann,

I recently bought a house at the beach. I'm a single woman and have always worked to support myself and put myself through school. This is my first home.

The problem is my married sister. She has let me know she is planning a two-week vacation with her husband and unruly kids in my new home. "Jeanette" has never worked in her life and did nothing to help me when I was struggling.

I do not want Jeanette and her family to come for two weeks. A weekend would be okay, but I don't feel like entertaining them, feeding them, and spending my vacation waiting on them. How do I tell her in a nice way?

Ann replied:

I assume English is your first language. Use it to tell Jeanette that you are not ready for guests yet and that you will let her know when you can accommodate visitors. Then invite her and the clan for a weekend when you feel you are up to it.

As you can see, Ann's suggestion is no-nonsense, direct, and to the point. It's free from unnecessary apologies or excuses. If you're like most women, you probably don't like the notion of saying a direct, unequivocal "No, I don't want to," or "No, that's not convenient," or one of its other variations. You might feel you have to have a better reason. Believe me, not wanting to do something is good enough reason not to do it. Saying "no" to an inconvenient or unreasonable request has an important advantage. It will permit you to feel empowered rather than resentful or annoyed for having allowed yourself to be put upon.

Saying no to our children in "need" may be extremely difficult. After all, a parent's inclination is to run to the rescue. In a March 30, 1997, *Miami Herald Sunday Magazine* article, columnist Ana

Veciana-Suarez wrote:

> I, like so many other parents, usually get involved in what I
> call search-and-rescue missions. We bail our children out
> instead of telling them, "Tough! You got yourself into this,
> now learn how to get yourself out of it."
> We do for our kids what they should do for themselves. We
> spell words for them instead of ordering them to the
> dictionary. And when they wait until the last minute to write
> their report on St. Augustine, we drive them to the library and
> stay up late that night coddling them along.
> We become a twenty-four-hour emergency service, devalu-
> ing our own time and needs. There is a difference between
> helping and becoming a child's doormat.

Ana makes a keen observation that applies in all situations. There
is a difference between helping and becoming someone's slave.
Women shouldn't devalue their own time and needs by saying
"yes" all the time. But they often do. Well, I encourage you to put
yourself first for a change!

It's helpful to be ready for those spur-of-the-moment situations
that take you by surprise. Have a variety of effective ways to say
"no" already on the tip of your tongue. Practice the many possible
forms of saying "no" suggested earlier in the chapter. Choose the
ones that work best for you.

### Seek Opportunities to Practice

Try the following suggestions to give yourself opportunities to
experience success with saying "no" in relatively nonthreatening
situations. Read through the list first. Begin with the suggestions
you find to be fairly innocuous. When you are comfortable saying
"no" in those situations, progress to those that are more difficult
for you.

1. The next time you're asked for your phone number by a store
   clerk while in the process of returning merchandise, say you
   don't care to provide the number and the return should be
   processed without it. It's unlikely you will have any resistance.

2. When a telemarketer disturbs you at home, why waste your valuable time listening to a lengthy sales pitch? If you are truly not interested, say so. You might add, "Please do not call me at home again." Keep in mind, you are not being impolite by refusing to allow unwanted callers to impose on your time.

3. Walk through the perfume section of a large department store. As the sales representatives attempt to spray you with their companies' samples, say "no thanks." If you're really adventurous, take it a step further with "Do you have a sample to give me so I might try it at home?"

4. Start saying "no" immediately. Practice saying no to inconvenient requests from your children, coworkers, friends, etc. Practice saying no to your friends' pets next time they attempt to jump on you. Get used to hearing the word come out of your mouth!

5. The next time you call a company and the operator asks, "Would you please hold?" say, "No, I don't want to hold!" What have you got to lose? The worst-case scenario is that you'll be put on hold anyway! Go for it. See what happens.

**EXERCISE**

Think of three situations where you wanted to say "no" but didn't. They might have involved inconvenient requests or suggestions to do things you would have preferred not to do.

*Example:* I wish I hadn't taken time away from an important project to drive two hours on a moment's notice to visit an acquaintance who was in town for just one night.

*Example:* I'm sorry I canceled my tennis game to drive my son to the library to finish a school project due the next day.

Now, consider how you could have assertively said no in each of the situations you identified. What you would have liked to have said?

*Example:* No, I can't make it, but thanks so much for your call. I'm working on a project, but I'll make every effort to see you next time you're in town. Please let me know in advance of your visit. I'd really like to get together.

*Example:* No, Jeremy. I can't take you to the library on such short notice. I already made plans to play tennis. Next time be sure to ask for my help several days before your assignment is due.

You no longer have to be a victim of circumstance. Practice saying your assertive responses aloud. Doesn't it feel great to please yourself for a change?

I know it is extremely difficult to use the assertive "no" if you're not used to it. At first, the words may just get stuck in your throat. That's okay. I promise it will become easier and easier. The natural high and boost to your self-esteem that you will experience as a result will be a powerful reward and the incentive you need. It's like using any new vocabulary word for the first time. Initially, it feels strange coming out of your mouth. You surreptitiously look around for listeners' reactions to see if anyone has noticed. Of course, no one ever has. After you make a conscious effort to use that new word several times in conversation, it will naturally become part of your vocabulary and roll off your tongue with ease. And so it is with saying "no"—or any of its possible forms. Give it a little time. Communicating assertively will soon become automatic and effortless.

# 5

# *Buy Time Before Responding*

Francine, a forty-year-old, first-time bride-to-be, was excited about marrying Nelson. In fifteen minutes, the minister was due to perform the ceremony. The guests were waiting for the bride and groom to appear. Nelson's attorney unexpectedly handed Francine a prenuptial agreement to sign. She was flabbergasted, since Nelson had not previously discussed this with her. Overcome with shock, Francine didn't know what to do. The attorney said, "Francine, the minister just arrived. Sign the papers. You don't want to keep the guests waiting now, do you?" Francine regained her composure, responding, "I need time to think about this. The guests will have to wait. Have Nelson inform them there will be no ceremony today."

Several days later, after much deliberation, Francine decided not to marry Nelson. She had wisely given herself time to consider the situation. Although the idea of a prenuptial contract was not offensive to her, she knew she would always resent Nelson for springing it on her at the eleventh hour.

Francine confided to me that she almost signed the prenuptial agreement and went through with the wedding because she was mortified by the thought of sending the guests home. But she also found she had misgivings about marrying someone who could pull such a callous and insensitive ploy. She knew she was really upset and needed time to calm down to consider the situation.

Francine would not allow herself to be pressured into making a decision she might regret for the rest of her life.

### *"I'll Think About It"*

The need to take time to consider options before committing to a decision applies to many situations. Friends or relatives' sudden requests, comments, or actions frequently take you by surprise. You may need time to think before committing yourself to a course of action.

When you're not ready to respond immediately, just say so. This is not a deliberate delaying tactic. You are not stalling to postpone asserting an unpopular decision. You are giving yourself time to better evaluate a situation and put your feelings into perspective.

Delaying your response will prevent you from making a commitment you may come to regret. It will help assure that you will feel good about yourself and your ultimate decision. Requesting time can be used when you've been criticized or challenged, not just when you have an important decision to make. If you feel your emotions are overpowering you, it's extremely reasonable to defer responding to consider the comments or criticism.

Renata chose to temporarily remain silent rather than react impulsively. She and Kyle were both assistant managers for a national chain of convenience stores. Kyle used every opportunity to insult Renata. He once goaded her with, "A moron could have done it better." Very angry, Renata was about to retort, "In that case, why didn't *you* do it?" However, she didn't want to say something she'd regret. She knew she'd have another opportunity to assert herself with Kyle and wanted to prepare for it.

The following week, Kyle was as nasty as ever at a company meeting. When Renata offered a suggestion about a new policy, Kyle snidely said, "Oh, that's a real winner of an idea." Renata used this opportunity to assert herself. "Kyle, please stop insulting me. You use every chance you get to put me down. What have I done to make you so hostile?"

Renata had originally considered fighting fire with fire but
ultimately chose not to. Had she given Kyle a taste of his own
medicine by impetuously responding in kind, their conflict would
have escalated. Fortunately, she had taken the necessary time to
consider her options and their consequences.

I know I tend to react without thinking when someone insults or
unfairly criticizes me. I'm generally overcome by emotions that
cause me to respond impulsively, often in a counterproductive way.
That's the moment when I must be sensible enough to keep my
mouth shut until I've had a chance to calm down. I must frequently
remind myself to follow my own advice whenever I'm angry or
upset.

There are many perfectly acceptable ways to ask for time in
order to best decide how to respond. Here are several options:

I'd like to think about that.
I'm not ready to make a decision right now.
I'll let you know what I decide.
I'm confused. I want to sort out my feelings before
    responding.
Let me think about what you've said and talk to you about it
    later.
I'm really upset right now. I need time to calm down before I
    reply.
You caught me by surprise. I need time to consider this
    before I answer.

### Use Your Head, Not Your Heart

Robert and I had been colleagues for years. The relationship had
been strictly professional until a strong attraction began developing between us. We were both divorced. However, Robert was
involved in a relationship from which he was not ready to extricate
himself. He invited me out to dinner and made it perfectly clear
we'd have to be discreet so that his girlfriend, Rebecca, wouldn't
find out.

My heart screamed "yes!" After all, Robert was attractive,
intelligent, attentive, and had a great sense of humor. And, he

wasn't married! Longing for romance, I reasoned no harm would be done. He and Rebecca would eventually terminate their situation and we'd be able to share an honest, open, relationship. However, deep down inside of me, a nagging doubt remained. I knew I needed time to think of a response I wouldn't later regret. I told Robert I'd meet him the next day and let him know. He pressed me, "I'm crazy about you. Why can't you tell me now?" Afraid I'd lose my resolve, I quickly left, calling over my shoulder, "I said I'll let you know tomorrow."

Fortunately, my good sense prevailed. I realized such a relationship was not in my best interest. I spent the evening carefully choosing and practicing the words I would say the next day. I said this: "Robert, I adore you. But I have too much self-respect to become involved with anyone who is unwilling to acknowledge me publicly to friends and family. If we still feel the same way about each other when you and Rebecca go your separate ways, we'll revisit this!"

We've all been faced with situations where our decisions are based on emotions rather than rational thoughts. We want something so badly, we refuse to acknowledge our gut feeling that something is not quite right. Aching for emotional satisfaction, we ignore our inner voice telling us, "You'll be sorry." Getting into the habit of buying time in these situations will help you sort out any mixed-up emotions. It will help you balance the differences between the emotional and rational sides of your brain. You will probably realize that what you think you want "now" is not what's best for you later.

While on vacation, Maureen and Tom were enticed to a time-share resort's marketing promotion with the promise of free gifts. They fell in love with the resort's amenities: freshwater and saltwater swimming pools, tennis courts, golf course, private beach, and so forth. They left four hours later, $7,000 poorer, the proud owners of a time-share unit they would never use.

What happened here? Maureen and Tom were temporarily taken in by the glitz and glamour of the resort. They ended up selling their "week" a few years later at a substantial loss. They allowed their emotions to overshadow logical, practical reasoning. Had they taken several days to think it over, they would have had time to consider the investment objectively. The couple would have determined that the disadvantages of owning at this particular location outweighed the advantages. They later realized that it was inconvenient and expensive to get to; they didn't want to be obligated going to the same place each year; and yearly maintenance and administrative fees were quite high.

Sometimes the desire for instant gratification often overshadows good judgment. When you take time to think before making a commitment, you avoid the need to kick yourself later for making a foolish choice.

Tom and Maureen should have deferred their decision until they had time to make a list of pros and cons regarding the purchase. Buying time before writing the check would have allowed them to reconcile the differences between their emotions and their rational thoughts.

### *Don't Be Pressured*

In the market for a new car, I spent hours one Saturday at a car dealership deciding which model to buy. Hal, the salesman, and I were seated at a table in one of those cubicles all dealerships seem to have. Hal quoted me a "special" price, reminding me it was the last car on the lot with the features I wanted. I loved the car and was tempted to close the deal on the spot. However, the little voice in my head told me to look around some more before making a decision. Hal stood up, towered over me, and declared, "You need to decide now. The special price is only good if you buy the car today. I can't offer you the same deal if you leave and come back." I, too, stood up, looked him in the eye, and assertively replied, "Thanks for your time, Hal. I don't do business that way and I don't like to be pressured. Goodbye." I ended up buying a less-expensive car that I liked even better at another dealership.

There are individuals who will not respect your need for time to consider your options. They will scoff at your desire to give a matter more thought before making a decision. These manipulators will try to pressure you into agreeing to their demands or proposal right away. Don't let them. Never feel you have to rush into a hasty decision or answer until you're good and ready.

It's also not uncommon for those in positions of authority to pressure you into a hasty decision by attempting to make you feel guilty. Mrs. Sawyer, the principal of an exclusive private school, recommended to Barbara and her husband, Brad, that their son, Phillip, repeat kindergarten. Mrs. Sawyer believed Phillip to be too socially and emotionally immature to go to first grade. Barbara and Brad wanted to consider the pros and cons of such an action before agreeing with the recommendations. Mrs. Sawyer wanted their decision by the following day, claiming the school's administration needed to plan enrollment caps for next year's kindergarten and first-grade classes. She warned them the school would not be responsible for Phillip's poor performance if he did not repeat kindergarten.

Barbara asked my opinion. Of course, she wanted to do what was best for her son. She didn't feel that Phillip was any less mature than any other six-year-old continuing to first grade. I encouraged her to get a second opinion from an independent child psychologist. She and Brad let Mrs. Sawyer know they would decide after Phillip was tested the following week, not before. Mrs. Sawyer acquiesced in the face of their justified assertiveness.

As it turned out, the psychologist strongly recommended Phillip wait the extra year to begin first grade. After all was said and done, Barbara and Brad ended up following Mrs. Sawyer's recommendation. The point is that they did not allow Mrs. Sawyer to pressure them into a quick response. By asserting themselves and taking the time necessary to get another opinion, they felt confident that their decision was the right one.

### Better Late Than Never

Twenty-five years ago, I was hired as an instructor in the speech department at the college where I still teach. At the dean's request, I gladly agreed to teach a course for the English as a Second Language department. I met with Walt, the chairman of that department. He treated me rudely, acting as if he were doing me a favor by allowing me to teach for him. I endured his arrogance in silence and left his office. Approximately five years ago, I found myself sitting next to Walt during a meeting. We engaged in pleasant, friendly conversation. I described his first meeting with me and how hurt I had been by his attitude. Walt was truly repentant. He couldn't apologize enough. We both laughed about it. I was finally free of the resentment I had harbored toward him for twenty years.

After graduating from medical school, Anita realized she preferred teaching. She loved her job as a high school biology teacher. At a family gathering, her Aunt Flo exclaimed, "Uncle Dave and I never dreamed you'd end up in a such a low paying job." Anita was insulted. Speechless, Anita walked away. For the next several days, she considered what she should have told Flo. Driving home from work one afternoon, Anita wished she had said, "I'm a great teacher, and I love what I do!"

Anita was so eager to finally break her silence that she phoned Flo that evening. She reminded Flo of the wisecrack and delivered her belated assertion. Flo offered a feeble apology and hung up. After a week of wondering "what she should have said," Anita felt great.

Many women believe they've lost their right to assert themselves if they don't do so immediately. They remain frustrated and annoyed with themselves for not having expressed their feelings about a situation that may have occurred weeks, months, or even years before. Please, refuse to believe that you've lost your chance for an appropriate assertion. Never feel that too much time has passed or that it's too late to do anything about it now. It's never too late to express your feelings, however delayed! It's never too late to feel better about yourself.

Expressing thoughts that you had once been too reticent to communicate will bring you a great sense of relief. You'll feel wonderful that you finally had the courage to assert them.

When Michael and his twin sister, Leslie, graduated from dental school, their estranged father, Al, sent them graduation gifts. Al sent Michael $1,0000; Leslie received $500. As Michael and Leslie intended to open a private practice together, Michael suggested they pool the funds and deposit them in a joint account. Leslie was devastated by her father's latest display of favoritism. She had always been hurt by it as a child, but she was never assertive enough to share her feelings. Three years later, she felt compelled to write her father a letter expressing how she felt. Leslie finally felt liberated and proud of herself for saying what she had always wanted to say.

As you can see, there's no need to suffer any longer from the "if only I'd said..." syndrome. It doesn't matter whether it's two days, two weeks, or twenty years after the fact. Write the letter. Make that call. Speak up! It's better late than never.

**EXERCISE**

Think of three situations in which you were annoyed with yourself for your lack of assertiveness. Describe the circumstance and formulate a *"what I should have said"* response.

*Example:* My friend Shannon had just recovered from cancer surgery. I drove with her from New Orleans to a world-renowned cancer research center in Texas for an evaluation of her condition. We asked the names of specific drugs that were to be used in Shannon's chemotherapy. The doctor condescendingly replied, "If I tell you, you won't remember anyway." Our mouths fell open. Neither of us could think of a response. The specialist said she'd send the recommendations to Shannon's oncologist in New Orleans. In the car on the way back to Louisiana, we thought of two good "what I should have said" comments.

I should have said: "We're very intelligent women and we have very good memories" or "Really, we're highly intelligent. You'd be amazed at what we can remember."

## It's Okay to Change Your Mind

Adrienne ran into her friend Sue unexpectedly at the bookstore. She showed Sue several travel brochures and a detailed itinerary of a cross-country tour she had booked. Sue expressed interest in joining the tour. Adrienne invited her to be her roommate, pointing out that the double-occupancy cost per person was significantly lower than the single-occupancy rate. Sue accepted. Several days later, Sue realized she had committed herself prematurely. She wasn't that crazy about the itinerary and didn't like the tour operator's choice of airlines. She decided not to go but dreaded telling Adrienne she had changed her mind. When she finally broke the news, Adrienne reacted graciously, "Don't worry about it. I'm glad you told me now rather than later. I still have time to find another roommate."

If you find you've reacted hastily, you have the right to change your mind! Unfortunately, many women hesitate to do so. They fear being considered indecisive or wishy-washy. It's perfectly normal to have second thoughts about a decision you've arrived at prematurely. Give yourself permission to alter it.

Lydia was extremely comfortable with her position as the head of customer service for a large computer corporation. She knew her job thoroughly. When there was an opening for director of Latin American sales, her boss convinced her to apply for the position. After all applications were in, Lydia decided she wasn't interested in the job. Although the position offered a significantly higher salary than she was currently earning, it involved longer hours and frequent travel which would take her away from her family. Not wanting to appear wishy-washy by admitting that she had changed her mind, Lydia didn't withdraw her application. She reasoned that she wouldn't be selected for the position anyway. Well, she was! Lydia was chosen over eleven other highly qualified candidates and then felt obligated to accept the promotion. As she feared, she was extremely unhappy in her new position. She begged out of it three weeks later.

Lydia had every right to change her mind and withdraw her application after submitting it. Had she announced her change of heart when she first wanted to, no one would have been inconvenienced. She would have spared herself much personal anguish and aggravation.

We've all been in situations where we've wanted to change our minds but hesitated to announce our intention to do so. Please believe that there is nothing wrong with changing your mind. The

key is that once you decide to do it, say so immediately. Procrastination only makes matters worse, as it did for Lydia. It's unfair
to the individuals affected by your decision, whereas it wouldn't
have been unfair had you told them earlier.

Changing your mind is not the same as breaking a promise. A
promise is a pledge to do or not to do something. It frequently
causes others to make plans they might not have made. It may
cause them to do something they wouldn't have done based on
their expectation that you will keep your vow. Breaking a promise
often unduly inconveniences one or more individuals. Except for
emergencies, or extreme circumstances, you should avoid breaking promises. And even then, a sincere explanation is in order. On
the other hand, changing your mind doesn't unjustly impact
someone else. The only person affected by your change of heart is
*you!*

For example, breaking your promise at the last moment to
babysit for a neighbor's children creates a problem for her. She
must now cancel her appointment, as she is unable to get a
replacement on such short notice. However, changing your mind at
the last moment to meet a group of friends for coffee doesn't
inconvenience anyone. Although they're likely to be disappointed,
they don't have to change their plans. They are able to follow
through with them as scheduled.

Taking time to consider a request will drastically reduce the
need to revise your decision later. But you're only human. We all
make hasty choices and have nagging doubts about them later.
We've all hung up the phone after agreeing to a friend's request,
thinking, "Why in the world did I say 'yes' and agree to do this?"
When this happens and you have misgivings about a response
you've given, there's no need to feel trapped. You have the right to
change your mind. Assert that right when necessary.

### Say "Yes" on Your Terms

Natalie had just recovered from a life-threatening illness, given up
her private practice as a speech pathologist, and moved to a new
city. She was anxious to return to work in her profession but was

reluctant to take on too much too soon. The local university offered her a full-time position supervising speech pathology practicum students. Natalie was concerned that a full-time position would be too taxing, as she hadn't fully regained her strength. Her prospective employer sensed she was about to decline the offer and said, "Look, Natalie, there's no need for an immediate decision. We'll be happy to work with you. Think it over."

Natalie discussed her health concerns with her husband and asked his opinion. He was positive that she would enjoy such a position and he didn't want her to dismiss the opportunity hastily. He encouraged her to say she'd accept the position if she could work just three days a week. Natalie mused, "You're right. I've got nothing to lose and everything to gain." The university agreed. The three-day schedule worked out perfectly for her, and several months later Natalie felt she was able to start working five days a week. Everyone was satisfied.

There will be times when an offer or request is basically agreeable but you're not 100 percent certain about it. Some aspect bothers you and you're not quite ready to say "yes" unconditionally. Assert your need "to think about it" before granting the favor or agreeing to the proposal. You have the absolute right and responsibility to yourself to change aspects of a proposition that make you uneasy.

"That sounds pretty good. Let me give it some thought" or "That seems like a good idea. I'd like to sleep on it before I let you know" are good expressions to use when you want to say "yes" but on your terms.

When Phyllis called from New York, she told her close friend Shelley, "Frank and I want to spend our vacation in Florida. May we stay at your house for two weeks? You'll hardly notice we're there. We'll have a rental car and will just come and go as we please. By the way, we don't want to leave Maxy in a kennel so we're bringing him along." Shelley thought about it for a couple of days. She knew from the start that she wanted her friends to visit, but she wasn't sure about their poorly trained dog. She decided she simply didn't want that animal in her house. Shelley called around and located a neigh-borhood kennel where Phyllis and Frank could board Maxy and visit

~~him until she really wanted to please her friends without sacrificing~~ her own needs. She would have been annoyed with herself had she allowed an unruly dog to run wild through her home. Shelley orchestrated a win-win situation by saying "yes" on her terms.

Saying "yes" on your terms won't always yield win-win situations as it did with Natalie and Shelley. In their book, *Stand Up, Speak Out, Talk Back!,* Alberti and Emmons state, "Sometimes your goals will be incompatible with the other person's. At times, others may be unreasonable or unyielding, and the best of assertions will be to no avail."

The university could have said, "Natalie, those are the terms of our offer. Take them or leave them." Phyllis could have told Shelley, "Love us, love our dog. Maxy goes where we go. I guess we won't be visiting."

Fortunately, neither of these scenarios occurred, but they could have. So be it! You can't please everyone all of the time. You'll usually find that your assertive communication works and pleases others as well as yourself. Just remember, you have the absolute right to request time to think about how you feel and what you want. Even if things don't turn out the way you hoped, you still have every reason to feel good about yourself and know you did the right thing.

### EXERCISE

Look at the following situations. Without taking time to think them through carefully, what would your immediate response be? Remember, don't think about them too much. What is the first response that occurs to you?

*Situation 1:* A friend asks you to pick her up at the airport. You're scheduled to attend a meeting at the same time her flight is due to arrive.

*Situation 2:* Your son wants to throw a surprise party for his best friend's eighteenth birthday at your house on Saturday night. He knows you have plans for that specific evening and won't be home to supervise. He begs you to let him have the party unsupervised.

*Situation 3:* Your daughter, who lives nearby, wants you, "grandma," to keep her three-year-old twins at your house for a week. She works from home and needs an uninterrupted opportunity to finish an important project. You were looking forward to several already planned evening social engagements with your friends.

Now look at the situations again and ask for time to think. Although you want to be as helpful as possible, some aspects of the requests need to be changed to better accommodate your own agenda. How might you say yes on your terms to the situations? Come up with a response that takes your feelings and needs into account before reading the other possible solutions given below.

*Possible solutions to Situation 1:* Ask your friend if she could possibly arrive on a later flight; suggest a place for her to wait and let her know you'll be happy to pick her up after your meeting; offer to pay her cab fare to your home or office where she could comfortably wait for you; advise her that you've asked someone else to pick her up.

*Possible solutions to Situation 2:* Allow your son to have the party on Friday night or Sunday; suggest that he throw the party the previous Saturday; allow him to have the party on the desired evening only if a trusted adult friend or family member is available to supervise.

*Possible solutions to Situation 3:* Offer to care for the children during the day only; agree to the request if your daughter will hire a baby-sitter for those evenings you'll be unavailable.

Be assured, making a hasty decision to please someone is seldom in your best interest. Requesting time to consider a response can help you reconcile the difference between your emotions and rational thoughts. It will prevent you from making a remark or commitment you may later regret. Postponing a decision because of a conscientious need to consider it more fully does not mean you are indecisive. A little more thought up front will yield much better feeling even further, it's rarely ever too late for an appropriate assertion. Feel free to express your feelings about a situation that bothered you even if it occurred months ago. And don't forget, if you become unhappy with a decision you've made, you always have the right to change your mind!

# 6

## "That's Not Acceptable"

After sightseeing all day in Paris, I returned to my hotel room to find my cash and traveler's checks stolen. When I called the company that issued the checks to report the theft, Matthew, a very pleasant customer service representative, told me to take a cab to their nearest office where I could pick up replacement checks. When I asked if he could have the checks delivered to my hotel, he informed me that was impossible. I was upset but managed to follow my own advice.

I responded, "That's not acceptable, Matthew. I just spent my last centime. I have no francs to take the Metro, let alone a cab!" "I'm sorry, Madam," Matthew said. "That's the best I can do. The office near your hotel is currently closed." I repeated, "Matthew, it's simply not acceptable that you won't deliver the checks to me personally. All my cash and traveler's checks were stolen. I have no money to take a cab. The company clearly advertises hand-delivered refunds, wherever you want, virtually anywhere in the world. I expect you to honor your commitment to your customers and deliver the checks to me at my hotel. I will be eternally grateful to you for arranging that!"

To my great relief, Matthew replied, "Madam, don't worry. You've made your point. I'm sorry for your inconvenience. I will have a courier deliver the checks to you within the hour." True to his word, a courier arrived with the checks an hour later.

### Persistence Pays

If you let them, some businesses and individuals will try to do what's easiest for *them,* not what's best for *you.* They will resort to the least time-consuming, least expensive way to satisfy your complaint. They don't want to inconvenience themselves or go to any expense if it isn't necessary. They think they can just throw you a little bone and you'll go away satisfied. The key is to be persistent and get what you're entitled to. Hold out for that bigger bone. Don't settle for less than you deserve. Don't give up so easily.

My dear friend Shannon lives in Gainesville, Florida. She flew into New Orleans on business and rented a car at the airport. When the engine developed a loud rattling sound the next day, Shannon called the car rental agency to request a different car be brought to her. She was told that she had to drive the car back to the airport herself. Shannon described the situation and mentioned she had been a loyal customer for years and wanted to continue to do business with the company. She was still told that she had to return the car herself. Shannon insisted upon speaking to the manager of the agency, and she told him, "It's not acceptable that your agency won't send someone to exchange my rental car. It's defective. The engine is making a loud rattling sound and the steering wheel vibrates. I'm afraid to drive it. It's outlandish to have me drive an unsafe car all the way back to the airport from downtown. I want someone from your office to bring me another car and take this one back. Otherwise, I'll leave this car in the garage where it's parked and mail you the keys." The manager reluctantly sent an employee to trade the faulty car for a good one.

In both situations, Shannon's and mine, the companies involved tried to take the easy way out at our expense. We simply wouldn't allow them to take advantage of our vulnerability. You can see from these two examples that it is possible to empower yourself and get what you're entitled to. You do, however, need to be persistent. Never feel like you're being a pest or a bother. You're simply looking out for your own best interests because it's obvious the "other guy" sure isn't! Persistence pays! Assert your rights. When you do, you'll find that things go your way more often than not.

### Ask for What You Want

Countless women feel helpless to object when they get less than they deserve or have a right to expect. They feel compelled to accept unfair treatment, shoddy workmanship, and poor service. You, too, might be reluctant to protest when you have every right to do so. As a result, you probably find yourself exploited or needless inconvenienced. Most women I know are tired of being treated like second-class citizens, but they don't know what to do about it. Remember Eve, the interior designer who asked, "Why do people walk all over me?" At the time I answered her, "Because you let them. People will treat you the way you teach them to treat you." I'd like to revise that advice for this chapter: "People will treat you the way you *ask* them to treat you!"

In the *Aladdin Factor,* coauthor Jack Canfield writes,

> Until I knew I could ask for what I wanted, I had lived my life in an unacknowledged state of resignation. I had silently agreed not to be a nuisance or a bother, to never intrude on anyone, to never take up anyone's time and certainly not to be a pest!
>
> I had settled for less than the best of everything—mediocre seats at plays and drafty seats at restaurants. Cold or badly prepared food was never sent back. I settled for substandard rooms in hotels and flew coach when I could have been upgraded to first class. I accepted shoddy workmanship and poor performance. I wore clothes that didn't fit perfectly and occasionally wore shoes that were too tight. ("Don't worry, they'll stretch.") I was afraid to return or exchange unwanted gifts, and I rarely, if ever, asked a salesclerk to help me find something I was looking for.

Jack Canfield didn't know he could say, "That's not acceptable." He didn't know he could ask for what he wanted or needed. He didn't know he could assert his right to be treated respectfully and

Fairly Well, he known to now As an internationally renowned speaker and best-selling author, he has devoted himself to encouraging others to ask for what they want, too.

Jean Baer, author of *How to Be an Assertive (Not Aggressive) Woman,* interviewed Barbara Walters while she was still cohost of *The Today Show,* over twenty years ago. She quotes Barbara as having said, "My professional life used to be full of opportunities I didn't get because I didn't ask for them. I've always been afraid I'd be thought too aggressive if I spoke up. Now, not only do I have confidence, but I realize the atmosphere all around me has changed and such things are possible."

Many women feel uncomfortable or even scared to say, *"That's not acceptable,"* and to ask for what they want. They're afraid of the risks involved. What are the risks? The risk of confrontation? The risk of rejection?

Remember, any attempt on your part to change the status quo involves risk. But if you're too timid to take the risk, you sell yourself short. For example, if you're afraid to risk asking a coworker to stop calling you "honey," or to risk asking your boss for a raise, or to risk telling the phone company you were charged for calls you didn't make, you are always the loser. When we avoid this type of risk-taking, we must live with that little voice we all have inside that criticizes us for our timidity. Our own inner critics continue to whittle away at our self-esteem. So, make asking for what you want a priority. As the title of Susan Jeffers's best-seller suggests, *Feel the Fear and Do It Anyway!* After all, what is there to be afraid of? That you won't get what you ask for? So what! You don't have it now. If your request is refused, you're no worse off than before you asked.

Haven't you ever heard about the old man who asked all the girls exiting a department store for a kiss? When an observer asked him if he was often rejected, the old man replied happily, "Of course, but I get lots of kisses, also!"

Asking for what you want takes patience and practice. Each time you do it, you may have to summon up your courage all over again. But it will become easier and easier. So do it regularly. You'll be glad you did!

I've outlined a simple approach for you to follow. It was inspired by the DESC (Describe Express Specify Consequences) scriptwriting technique described by Sharon Anthony Bower and Gordon H. Bower in their book, *Asserting Your Self.* Try it whenever your first attempt to get what you're entitled to is unsuccessful.

1. Assert your position that the response you've received is unacceptable.
2. Describe the situation briefly.
3. Justify your request.
4. Ask for what you want.
5. State the positive consequences that will occur if your request is granted, and/or
6. State the negative consequences that will occur if your request is denied. (Use this only as a last resort.)

Let's return to my stolen traveler's checks experience and analyze how the approach worked there.

"Matthew, that's simply not acceptable that you won't deliver the checks to me personally." (I asserted my position that Matthew's response was unacceptable.)

"All my cash and traveler's checks were stolen. I have no money." (I described the situation.)

"Your company clearly advertises hand-delivered refunds, wherever you want, virtually anywhere in the world." (I justified my request.)

"I expect you to honor your commitment to your customers and deliver the checks to me at my hotel." (I asked for what I wanted.)

"I will be eternally grateful to you for arranging that!" (I stated the consequence of my request being granted.)

Shannon also followed the same basic approach in her dealings with the manager of the rental car agency.

"That's not acceptable that your agency won't send someone to exchange my rental car." (She asserted that the employee's response was unacceptable.)

"It's dangerous. The engine is making a loud rattling sound and the steering wheel vibrates." (She described the situation.)

"I'm afraid to drive it. It's not safe. It's outlandish to expect me to drive an unsafe car all the way back to the airport from downtown." (She justified her request.)

"I want someone to bring me another car and take this one back." (She asked for what she wanted.)

"Otherwise, I'll just leave this car in the garage where it's parked and mail you the keys." (She stated the consequence of her request being denied.)

It won't always be necessary to use all six steps in this approach. Most of the time, people will give you what you want as soon as you speak up and ask them to. Go ahead and try it. You're likely to be pleasantly surprised.

When my son's godmother, Tommie, visited from Arizona, we went to an elegant South Miami Beach restaurant for lunch. The waiter, Marcus, mentioned that all beverages were included in the price. As we ordered dessert, Marcus asked if we'd like cappuccinos also. Thinking they were included in the luncheon price, we chimed, "Of course!" We each had two! Upon receiving the bill, we saw we had been charged thirty dollars for them. Tommie brought the "error" to Marcus's attention. He replied, "Oh, that's not an error. When I said beverages, I only meant soft drinks or mineral water." Tommie nicely persisted, "Lunch was lovely and the service was fabulous. However, had we known the cappuccinos were $7.50 each, we wouldn't have ordered them. I think you should deduct them from the bill." Marcus graciously apologized, "You're absolutely right. Please forgive me. The cappuccinos are on the house."

Tommie and I were treated courteously and fairly. All Tommie had to do was describe the problem and ask for what she wanted.

Kristi ordered enlargements of several photographs at a local photo shop. The lab mistakenly made them 5" × 7" instead of the larger size she wanted. When she brought the error to the technician's attention, he said the order form showed she requested 5" × 7"s and she'd have to pay for them. Kristi spoke up:

"The person who wrote up the order must have made a mistake. I ordered 10″ × 12″ photographs, not 5″ × 7″s. Please have them redone. I'll be happy to pay you for the 10″ × 12″s." He then apologized for the error and had the lab make the enlargements Kristi wanted. In this situation, all Kristi had to do was briefly point out the problem and ask for it to be resolved. A longer explanation was not necessary. However, had the technician insisted that she pay for the 5″ × 7″ photographs, a "That's not acceptable," response would have been very helpful. Here's how Kristi could have responded if he had given her a hard time:

"Expecting me to pay for the 5″ × 7″ enlargements is not acceptable." (Assert your position that the response you've received is unacceptable.)

"The lab made a mistake. I ordered 10″ × 12″ enlargements and received smaller ones instead." (Describe the situation.)

"I shouldn't be charged for someone else's mistake. It's not my fault that the clerk who took my order wrote the wrong information." (Justify your request.)

"I would like you to redo these pictures and make me the 10″ × 12″s I wanted." (Ask for what you want.)

"I will be happy to pay for the 10″ × 12″s and bring all my film here to be developed in the future." (State the positive consequences that will occur if your request is granted.)

Diane, a student of mine, received an unfair bill from a roofing company. Mr. Manning, the owner of the company, examined her leaky roof and gave her a written estimate of $450 to fix it. Miguel, the roofer who made the repairs, told Diane the problem was less severe than Mr. Manning had thought. It was unnecessary to replace any of the tiles after all. Miguel completed the work quickly and competently. Diane called the company and meekly asked if they would adjust her bill to reflect the actual work done. Mrs. Manning, the office manager, insisted she pay the full $450. Diane was upset and asked my advice. I encouraged her to read a draft of this chapter, formulate a "That's not acceptable" response, and call the roofing company back. I gave her the six-step approach to use as a guide. Here's what Diane came up with:

"Your refusal to reduce my bill is not acceptable." (Assert that the situation is unacceptable.)

"The roofer didn't have to replace any tiles. Less work was done than described in the estimate." (Describe the situation.)

"The roof repair was less involved than originally thought. Mr. Manning included the cost of replacing roof tiles in his original estimate. It's unethical to ask me to pay for work that wasn't done." (Justify your response.)

"I want you to adjust my bill and charge me only for the actual work done." (Ask for what you want.)

"Your roofer was very professional. I'd like to recommend your company to others." (State the positive outcome that will occur if your request is granted.)

"I will not send you anything until my lawyer advises me what to do. Furthermore, I intend to call the Better Business Bureau." (State the negative consequences that will occur if your request is denied.)

The upshot was that Mrs. Manning was inflexible and adamant that Diane pay the full amount. Diane insisted on speaking to Mr. Manning. He, too, had no intention of granting Diane's justified request until she stated her negative consequence. Upon hearing it, he immediately agreed to reduce the bill to $350.

## A Word About Consequences

It's always best to think positive! Assume your request will be granted and emphasize the positive consequences that will result. For example, an employee asking for a raise might finish with, "I'm looking forward to working here for many years." A homeowner asking the cable company to fix his broken TV cable immediately might state, "My family will be most appreciative; I hope to remain a customer of yours" or "I expect to recommend your company to my neighbors." Or, as I told Matthew, "I will be eternally grateful to you for arranging that!" Promising someone your appreciation or loyalty before he does what you ask often motivates that person to satisfy you. He either has a genuine desire to make you happy or wants you to feel grateful to him for doing you a "favor." Don't believe for a moment that the individual is doing you any favors. He's just doing what he should have done for you to begin with. In either case, whatever that person's motivation for granting your request shouldn't matter to you. The main thing is that you get what you're entitled to. Just smile, say thanks, and be on your way!

When possible, avoid stating a consequence negatively. Instead of getting you what you want, it can seem like an ultimatum and cause the other person to become defensive or resentful. Whenever you can, it's always better to state your consequence in positive terms. The negative consequence is frequently implied anyway. For example, "If you exchange this defective product, I will continue to shop here" implies that if the owner doesn't exchange the product, you will never shop in that store again. Kristi's response, "I'll be happy to pay for the 10″ × 12″ enlargements and bring all my film here to be developed," implies that she won't pay for the 5″ × 7″s and that she'll bring her film elsewhere in the future.

Although stating a consequence in negative terms should be avoided, sometimes it's absolutely necessary. Shannon and Diane, for example, had no other recourse. They had exhausted all other possibilities for receiving fair treatment. Stating the negative consequences that would occur if their justified requests were denied was their last resort. It wasn't until Shannon announced her intention to leave the car where it was, and Diane threatened to call the Better Business Bureau, that they got what they wanted.

**EXERCISE**

How would you ask for what you want in the following situations? (Refuse to allow yourself to be unfairly treated or inconvenienced. Use the same six-step approach format that Diane used as a guide to formulating your response.)

*Situation:* Your dog's paw has been swollen for several days. Your veterinarian, Dr. Winnig, probes it with his fingers, tells you it's a tumor, and recommends surgery. You take your pet to another veterinarian for a second opinion. He removes a large thorn embedded in your dog's paw. There was no tumor. You advise Dr. Winnig of his error. He still bills you $45 for the office visit.

Assert that the situation is unacceptable:

Describe the situation:

Justify your request:

Ask for what you want:

State the positive outcome that will occur if your request is granted:

State the negative consequences that will occur if your request is denied:

*Situation:* Ned, a technician at a computer repair center, called to advise you that your computer would be ready for pickup anytime after 1:00 P.M. When you arrive at 3:00 P.M., he's busy showing another customer how to play a computer game. Although your computer has been ready for two hours, Ned asks you to wait approximately twenty-five minutes so he can finish what he's doing. You explain that you're in a hurry as you have to pick up the kids from school and get to an appointment. He suggests you go do your errands first and come back for your computer anytime before 6.00 P.M.

Assert that the situation is unacceptable:

Describe the situation:

Justify your request:


Ask for what you want:


State the positive outcome that will occur if your request is granted:


State the negative consequences that will occur if your request is denied:


*Situation:* Before leaving on vacation, you contract with a painter to paint the exterior of your house while you're gone. You select the paint and negotiate a price that fits your budget. You return to find that he used a slightly different shade than the one you specified. Fortunately, you like it a lot and are willing to accept it. The painter informs you that you owe him an extra $300 because he used a more expensive paint. When you protest, he shows you his invoice confirming he really did use a higher quality paint. He insists you pay him the additional money.

Assert that the situation is unacceptable:


Describe the situation:


Justify your request:


Ask for what you want:


State the positive outcome that will occur if your request is granted:

know the negative consequences that will occur if your request is denied:

*Situation:* Describe your own "That's not acceptable" situation. It should be one that you've personally experienced. How did you handle it at the time? Use the six steps to imagine how you would handle it now.

## Learning to Ask

As you can see by the examples described in this section, other people won't automatically do what's right and treat you fairly unless you ask them to. But when you do ask, they are often quite gracious and willing to accommodate you. Asking for what you want has many benefits. It helps you feel good about yourself for speaking up and gives others a chance to do the right thing, not to mention it frequently gets you what you want! Sometimes, others really want to help you but don't know how. You need to tell them.

For example, all Kristi had to do was tell Eric she wanted her photographs redone, and he had them redone. All Tommie had to do was ask Marcus to deduct the price of the cappuccinos from our bill, and he deducted it. Remember, "In life, you don't get what you deserve, you get what you ask for!" You certainly won't get what you don't ask for. I learned that lesson the hard way!

The night before I checked out of a hotel where I had been staying, I learned that breakfast was to have been included in the room rate. No one had informed me about this perk when I arrived four days earlier. Not knowing that I had been entitled to daily complimentary breakfasts at the hotel, I had been eating at a diner down the street. I asked the reception clerk on duty, "Why didn't someone tell me I was entitled to a complimentary breakfast each morning?" The reply? "Because you didn't ask!"

On another occasion, I bought expensive computer equipment at a local computer superstore. I later overheard a student talking about the 15 percent discount she had received when she bought her computer there. She explained that all full-time students and teachers are eligible for the discount. I paid full price for my computer system not knowing I could have received an educator's discount. The store clerks never thought to tell me, and I hadn't asked!

So ask, ask, ask! You're not limited to asking for what you were specifically promised or entitled to either. Ask for anything you want. Ask about discounts, ask about complimentary breakfasts, ask about available perks, ask to speak to the manager, ask for better seats, ask for a table by the window, just ask! There's really no down side. The worst case scenario is that you'll be refused. So what? Speak up! Be persistent! Ask for what you want. You have nothing to lose by asking and everything to gain!

### Be Prepared to Walk Away

Linda, a college professor, wasn't afraid to protest when she was treated unfairly. She refused to accept less than she had been promised. When Mac, the academic dean at the college where Linda taught, asked her to become an interim assistant dean for six months, she wasn't that anxious to do it. However, she agreed because it was only temporary and it would be a good experience for her. Because Mac wanted to avoid the administrative hassle of increasing Linda's salary and then having to adjust it back to her normal teaching salary six months later, he agreed to give her a four-day work week and travel funds to attend an out-of-town professional conference later that year as an alternative to a salary increase.

A week later, Linda received a memo outlining the terms of her new position. When Linda commented that there was no mention of the four-day work week, Mac replied, "Well, I thought about it, but I can't give that to you." Linda quickly reminded him of their discussion: "I accepted this position based on our agreement. I was planning to take Fridays off." Mac looked down at his fingernails. "That's the way it's going to be, Linda. Take it or leave it." Linda looked directly at him, "Okay, in that case, I'll leave it."

Surprised that she was prepared to walk away, Mac offered Linda every other Friday off, but she wasn't interested. She thanked him for his "concession" and told him she'd rather go back to her first love, willing. The exasperated dean finally looked up. "Look, I'm willing to compromise. Like I said, you can have every other Friday off. You've got to meet me halfway." Linda wouldn't be thrown off track and firmly stated, " I shouldn't have to compromise. It's not acceptable for you to expect me to. You promised me a four-day work week every week. It was very clear. I would like you to live up to your end of our agreement." Mac did and Linda took the position.

Linda had the confidence to object when Mac attempted to change the terms of the understanding they'd reached. She was fully prepared to walk away from the position and feel good about it. She knew she would have kicked herself later had she accepted less than she wanted and had been promised. Fortunately, that turned out to be unnecessary.

Betty spent all afternoon at the cellular phone store asking questions, evaluating the different phone models, reading the contract and service agreement documents, filling out forms, and finally choosing a phone. She was ready to pay and be on her way. She was unprepared for the $50 programming charge the salesman told her about as she handed him her credit card. Surprised, Betty mildly protested, "You never told me about any programming charge. There's no mention of one in the contract either." The salesman glibly responded, "That's our policy. Everyone pays it. No one ever complains." Betty paid it and was annoyed with herself later.

We've all had experiences similar to Betty's. Haven't you ever expected to receive a particular item or service, and all of a sudden, what you get is not what you were promised, or, at the last minute, a new condition that you hadn't been told about up front suddenly gets thrown at you? All too often, women give in to a situation they're not happy about because they're caught off guard. They feel stuck and don't know what to say. That's exactly what happened to Betty.

Betty still wishes she had rejected the programming charge. She promised herself she'd speak up the next time, fully prepared to say, "The additional charge is not acceptable. It was not part of our agreement and you never mentioned it before now. If you insist on charging hidden fees, I'll take my business somewhere else."

Betty wants to state her consequence in strong, no-nonsense language. She wants to make it perfectly clear that she simply won't do business with anyone who resorts to springing hidden charges on customers at the last moment. She relishes the opportunity to walk away as her way of saying goodbye and good riddance.

You have a right, as Betty now realizes, to reject unexpected conditions when they are imposed on you. Sure it's a nuisance to forget the whole thing and go elsewhere. You don't want to just abort the mission after you've invested all that time and emotional energy in it. But it's often worth the inconvenience. It may cause some people to rethink their unfair practices and to be more straightforward with others in the future. Besides, being able to walk away from an unfair situation will give you marvelous feelings of empowerment and self-respect. Try it and you'll see what I mean.

Another time when you should be prepared to say "That's not acceptable" and walk away is when you don't receive exactly what you want and are paying for it. Why should you settle for second best when you expect and deserve the top of the line?

Ellen needed two copies of her 240-page doctoral dissertation. "I need the copies to look really good," she told Claudia, an employee at the photocopy center. "Not a problem," Claudia assured her. "They'll be perfect." Ellen returned for her copies and found small black smudges on all the pages. When she politely asked Claudia to redo the job, Claudia informed Ellen she would first have to pay for the two sets of copies already made. "I shouldn't have to pay for the bad copies. They look terrible. You assured me the job would be perfect," Ellen protested. "I never said that the copies would be perfect," Claudia insisted defensively. Ellen stood her ground, "I shouldn't have to pay for bad copies. I need them to look crisp and clean. You assured me that they would be perfect. I'd like you to redo them. If you can't do that, please let me speak to the manager. I have no intention of paying for these unacceptable copies." The manager assessed the situation and wisely replied, "Of course, we'll redo your copies at no extra charge. We'd like to keep you as a customer."

Ellen was fully prepared to walk away if she didn't receive satisfaction. Fortunately, she handled the situation beautifully and didn't have to take her business elsewhere. When Claudia insisted, "I never said the copies would be perfect," Ellen sensibly avoided replying, "Yes, you did." Engaging in a "No, I never said that/Yes you did," or "That's not what you said/Yes it is," or "I said thus and so/ No you didn't" debate creates a no-win situation. Steer clear of this type of discussion if you can. It rarely leads to a productive solution to your complaint or problem. Instead, do as Ellen did. Assert your position, ask for what you want, and if necessary, be prepared to walk away!

There is absolutely no reason you should ever feel obligated to accept unfair treatment from people whether they be plumbers, waitresses, lawyers, or doctors. It's your absolute right to say "That's not acceptable" and walk away from anyone who doesn't treat you fairly and respectfully.

In *How to Be an Assertive (Not Aggressive) Woman,* author Jean Baer describes women's basic inalienable rights. Two of these rights are the "right to expect others to treat you with dignity and to treat yourself the same way" and the "right to reject impossible situations." She writes, "In my own case I stuck with a famous gynecologist for years, even though he constantly broke appointments and sometimes failed to show up for them. He would also scream at me. I resented it but didn't think I had the right to pass judgment on someone so well known." She never left him as a patient until she was forced to; he died from drug withdrawal!

Jean Baer had every right to tell her gynecologist that his behavior was unacceptable and reject him as her doctor. She never did, but wished she had. So don't wait until someone who treats you disrespectfully has to die before you unplug from them. Let them know that their behavior is unacceptable. If they don't start treating you with dignity and respect now, be prepared to walk away from them and take your business elsewhere!

## A Word About Compromising

There will be times when someone asks you to compromise and you shouldn't have to. The terms of the understanding were very clear. After all, you both had an agreement, and suddenly the person creates new rules in the middle of the game and expects you to go along with them. Then, when you summon up your courage to object, that individual hits you with another whammy! He tries to manipulate you into settling for less than you expected by cajoling, "All right, I'll compromise if you will." Well, you are under no obligation to compromise. This is totally up to you. Just take time to consider if compromising is in your best interest. Decide whether what you get in return is worth it. If it is, compromise. If it isn't, don't. Why accept less than you expected and were promised? Stick to your guns, adopt an "It's all or nothing attitude," as Linda did with the dean. You want it all, as promised, or you don't want any of it!

If you do refuse to compromise, be prepared for confrontation. The confronter will frequently try to make you look as if you're the one who's being unreasonable. Expect to hear such comments as:

> Don't be so unreasonable.
> You've got to give a little to get a little.
> I'm willing to compromise.
> You should meet me halfway.
> I'll tell you what, I'll split the difference with you.
> Don't be so inflexible.
> You've got to bend a little.

Don't be sidetracked by the confronter's bluster. Be prepared to assert yourself with a "That's not acceptable" response as Linda did when Mac said, "Look, I'm willing to compromise. You've got to meet me halfway."

If you've ever been car shopping, you'll sympathize with what happened to Josh, a freshman at the University of Miami. Josh's grandmother gave him $10,000 to buy his first car. After conducting an exhaustive search, he decided to look at a 1992 Toyota Camry advertised in the paper. The owner, Greg, quoted him a price of $10,000. After test-driving the car, Josh fell in love with it. He told Greg he would buy it after he had it checked out. Aside from recommending new front tires, a mechanic gave the Camry a clean bill of health. Josh returned to Greg's house ready to finalize the deal when Greg pulled the rug out from under him. Greg upped his price to $11,000, suggesting Josh ask his grandmother for more money. Josh shook his head saying, "$11,000 is too much for that car," and he turned to leave. Greg quickly countered, "Wait a minute. Let's compromise and split the difference. Give me $10,500." Upset and disappointed, Josh mumbled, "Just forget it," and walked away.

The six-step approach for asserting "That's not acceptable" works particularly well in this type of situation. Here's how Josh might have used the approach with Greg:

> "Changing the price on me now is unacceptable. I shouldn't have to compromise." (Assert your position.)
> "You quoted me a price of $10,000. After a mechanic said the car was fine, you increased the price to $11,000." (Describe the situation.)
> "It's extremely unfair of you to change the terms of our agreement. You promised to sell me the car for $10,000 and I promised to buy it after a mechanic checked it out. I was ready to live up to my end of the agreement." (Provide justification.)
> "I expect you to live up to your end of the understanding and sell me the car for $10,000 as you promised. (Ask for what you want.)
> "Otherwise, I'll just find someone else to deal with. I'm sure I'll find another car I like." (State your consequence.)

Josh gave up too easily. Before walking away, he could have tried the "That's not acceptable" approach. Although it may not have gotten him the Camry for the $10,000, he would have felt good about himself for having had the gumption to speak up about an unjust situation.

Both Linda and Josh refused to compromise and accept less than they expected. They were both prepared to walk away. As it turned out, it was not necessary for Linda to do so. Of course, there are times when you might want to compromise. Maybe you don't want to walk away. Maybe the individual is willing to give you something else in place of what you were promised. Maybe you really don't mind making some concessions or sacrificing some of what you wanted. That's okay. Then compromising is great. You should do it. Read on to learn how to negotiate a compromise that works for you!

## *Negotiate* Is Just a Fancy Word for *Compromise*

If you shudder when you hear the word "negotiate," you're typical of many women. "Negotiate? I could never do that" you might think. Although you may feel that negotiating is beyond you, it really isn't. You already know the ropes. You negotiate all the time and do it very well.

*You negotiate with your kids:* "If you finish your dinner, we'll go out for ice cream," or "If you get an "A" in math, I'll take you to Disney World."

*Your kids negotiate with you:* "If you let me watch an extra hour of TV tonight, I'll clean my room tomorrow instead of Friday."

*You negotiate with your spouse:* "I'll go to football games with you, if you'll take tennis lessons with me."

*You negotiate with friends:* "I'll drive the kids to school in the morning, if you pick them up in the afternoon."

"Negotiate" just means "compromise," and you compromise all the time. After all, life is a series of compromises or negotiations. Think of it this way, and you'll be able to negotiate with ease.

Assuming you've already used the six-step "That's not acceptable" approach, and asked for what you want politely and assertively, the other party might react in one of two ways. He might agree to live up to his end of the agreement and give you what you expected—as Mac did with Linda and the copy center manager did with Ellen— or he might reject your request, as Greg did with Josh. Now you have a decision to make: to walk away or not. Let's say you don't want to walk away and you're willing to compromise to get what you want. Well, then, it's time to negotiate.

## *Deciding on Your Options*

Women frequently limit themselves to the idea that they have only two options to choose from: the "take it'" or "leave it" option. They forget to think about other possibilities. Where do these other possibilities come from? They come from you. You must create them. How? By asking for something in return. Make a list of several things you can ask for in exchange for giving in or making some concession. Then you'll be able to choose what you want in return for sacrificing some of what you were promised.

For example, you take your computer monitor in to be fixed early Friday morning and are promised it will be ready at 5:00 P.M. You emphasize your need to use it over the weekend and are doubly assured it will be fixed on time. When you return for your monitor, you're told, "We're so sorry. We forgot all about your job. Leave it over the weekend and we'll fix it first thing Monday morning." What do you do?

First, take time to consider the situation and generate some alternatives for yourself. You could wait until Monday to have your monitor fixed. You could become righteously indignant and take it somewhere else. You could ask the technician to work late to fix your monitor. You could request a loaner to use until yours is repaired. You could ask for a 50 percent discount on the repair bill to compensate you for your inconvenience. You could even suggest that your monitor be repaired for free!

Think about Josh and the Toyota for a moment. Let's say he really wants it, and he is willing to make some concessions to get it. What are some of his options? He could counteroffer $10,100 or any amount less than the $10,500 Greg claims he wants. He could ask Greg to let him pay off the additional amount over a six-month period. Josh could ask Greg to replace the two bad tires and/or the stained floor mats. He could ask Greg for a warrantee on the car against any mechanical failures for a twelve-month period.

There are any number of possibilities that might work for you in a similar situation. You are never limited to just one or the other.

### EXERCISE

In each of the following situations, the relevant parties are either unwilling or unable to abide by the terms of an agreement you reached with them. Rather than "walk away," you are willing to negotiate a compromise. What could you ask for in return for giving up some of what you expected and wanted? Take a few moments to consider each situation and generate a list of alternatives for yourself.

*Situation:* You arrive at the airport way in advance of your scheduled flight. You have a confirmed reservation but are told that the flight is overbooked and there is no seat for you on the plane. The airline promises you a seat on a flight five hours later. *What are some options you could suggest to the airline?*

*Situation:* You go to pick up a rental car in a foreign country. The specific make and model you reserved and wanted is not available. There are no comparable cars on hand in the same price range. *What are your options?*

*Situation:* You booked a cruise months in advance on condition that you would be assigned to the late dinner seating. You made it absolutely clear you didn't want the early seating. The day before you're to embark, your travel agent notifies you that you've been switched to the early dinner seating. She apologizes and claims a computer snafu. *What are your options?*

*Situation:* The week before a big party you've been planning, your caterer tells you she underestimated her costs for the menu you both decided upon. She now tells you that the appetizers and entrees you selected are going to cost $300 more than she originally indicated. *What are your options?*

*Situation:* You reserved a double room with a balcony overlooking the ocean. When you arrive at the hotel, there are no ocean view double rooms available. The manager gives you the choice of a suite that costs twice as much or a cheaper room overlooking the parking lot. *What are your options?*

### Choose the Best Alternative

Before you can choose the best alternative, you have to figure out what you want. How far are you willing to compromise? What's the minimum you're willing to accept? What are your targets and goals? Basically, what is your bottom line? You must sort all this out in your mind before you attempt to negotiate. Remember Linda and Mac? Linda knew she absolutely wanted every Friday off. For her, this was nonnegotiable. She may have been willing to give up something else to get the position, but the four-day work week was her bottom line. She would gladly walk away from the position rather than have to work on Fridays.

Consider the computer monitor situation. What would your bottom line be? In my case, I'd be willing to accept either the free use of a loaner monitor until mine was repaired or a completely "gratis" repair job. I'd prefer to take my business elsewhere rather than settle for any other option. If you hadn't planned on using your computer over the weekend, you might be perfectly willing to return for the monitor on Monday. That's your decision. If you are happy with it, that's all that matters. Just establish the situation in your own mind, and determine how far you're willing to compromise.

### Choosing Not to Walk Away

As you have seen, agreements with people break down all the time. Your best efforts to negotiate and make concessions may still fail to resolve the problem in your favor. Although you'd like to take your business elsewhere, it may be more of a nuisance than it's worth. Sometimes you've invested too much time and energy in a situation to simply walk away. You're willing to accept the unacceptable because of the hassle involved in starting over from scratch. Fine, that's a perfectly reasonable choice.

But the other side doesn't have to know that you feel that way, not at first anyway! Conceal your real intentions for the time being. Let the other party think you're going to discontinue the relationship if you don't get what you want. So go ahead and negotiate. You're likely to get more than you were actually willing to accept.

When Brittany developed a chronic skin problem, her dermatologist prescribed antibiotics and insisted Brittany see her on a monthly basis. This went on for eight months when it became clear the only reason she wanted to see Brittany each month was to bill the insurance company for an office visit. Dr. Jackobs balked when Brittany asked instead for a refillable prescription. "No," Dr. Jackobs insisted, I must see you monthly." Brittany was sorely tempted to tell her, "For what? All you do is rush in the room, hand me a new prescription and rush out wordlessly." Instead, Brittany negotiated, "Dr. Jackobs, at least make my prescription refillable three times." The dermatologist compromised by allowing one refill. Realizing this was the best she was going to get, Brittany said, "Thanks, see you in two months."

One refill of her prescription wasn't what Brittany wanted or thought was reasonable under the circumstances. She was tempted to walk away but didn't want the hassle of having to find a new dermatologist and explain her problem all over again. Brittany eventually did switch doctors when it was more convenient for her to do so.

Regina contracted to lease a bright red Jeep. She gave the saleswoman, Helen, a $1,000 deposit to order it. When Helen notified her that the Jeep had been delivered, Regina eagerly arrived expecting to drive away in her new red vehicle. Except it wasn't red; it was white! Helen apologized profusely, "I did everything I could but there were no red Jeeps with the features you wanted. This was the only one I could get you." Regina felt trapped. She had just sold her old car and needed another one immediately. She had her heart set on the red one but didn't want the aggravation of having to start looking for another car somewhere else. Fully intending to settle for the white Jeep and ultimately go through with the deal, Regina bluffed to see if she could win a concession or two. "In that case," Regina asserted, "please return my deposit. I really want a red car." Helen immediately offered, "I'll tell you what, if you take the white Jeep, we'll service it free for the life of the lease." Feeling really empowered now, Regina figured she had nothing to lose by asking for another concession. She negotiated further. "If you'll also agree to provide me with a free loaner car while mine is in for service, I'll accept the white Jeep." Helen presented Regina's proposal to her manager, who reluctantly wrote the new terms into the contract.

Both Brittany and Regina were willing to accept less than they wanted. They were willing to make concessions to avoid the aggravation of walking away from situations in which they had already invested a lot of time and energy. But they kept their intentions to themselves. Dr. Jackobs and Helen never knew that Brittany and Regina were willing to accept the unacceptable if their requests were not granted. Brittany and Regina created choices for themselves and asked for concessions in return for sacrificing what they wanted. The other sides felt compelled to compromise. In other words, Brittany and Regina negotiated, asked for something in return, and got more than they had been willing to accept.

Those three priceless words, "That's not acceptable," will empower you with feelings of courage and self-confidence. They can do so much to right the wrong situation! Saying them with a firm statement of your expectations works more often than not. They have come to my rescue on countless occasions. They'll work for you, too. (And if they don't, so what? What have you lost?) You still have choices. If the six-step approach for getting what you want fails to do the trick, you can always walk away. You're not obligated to settle for second best. Nor are you required to accept the unacceptable or compromise—unless you want to. If you want to walk away, walk away! And if you want to negotiate, negotiate! Just remember, if you decide to accept less than you've been promised, be sure to ask for something in return. The key is to decide what you want. Only you can make that decision for yourself!

# 7

# *Speak for Yourself*

I accompanied my divorced friend Marla when she brought her car in for repair. The shop manager gave her an oral estimate and offered a 10 percent discount if she left her car to have the work started that same day. I was distressed to hear these words pour from Marla's mouth, "My *husband* said you should give me a written estimate. He wants me to get a couple of other estimates before I make a decision. I know he's going to think yours is a bit high, even with the discount."

Marla was not even married, yet she created a fictitious husband to lend "authority" to her words. I'm sure you, too, have heard other women react in such ways as:

My *husband* says I shouldn't pay more than $200 to fix the stove.
My *father* wants a second opinion.
My *boss* thinks this procedure will waste too much time.
My *boyfriend* says I don't need a TV with all those features.

Many women diminish the value and importance of their thoughts and feelings by projecting them onto a third party—usually a man.

They believe that crediting a boyfriend, husband, or boss gives more power or credibility to their words. What happened here? What causes so many women to submerge their own identities in this way? Frequently, they have had past experiences with people who caused them to feel their words and ideas are worthless.

Lila grew up hearing her father say, "Women don't know anything." Her older brother followed his father's cue. He frequently teased Lila, "What do you know? You're a girl."

Andrea, director of admissions for a large hospital, went car shopping. One salesman refused to speak with her, saying, "Talking to you alone is a waste of time. You'll probably tell me you have to discuss it with your husband before making a decision." Another car salesman suggested, "Why don't you come back with your husband? Then we'll talk." Andrea was so intimidated, she "borrowed" a friend's husband to accompany her the next time she visited an automobile dealership.

With such unpleasant experiences as these, it's no wonder Lila and Andrea have such little confidence in themselves. This lack of self-assurance causes women to feel their words aren't worthy of the same respect as they would be if they were spoken by a man.

Much of your sense of personal power comes from your ability to express yourself with confidence. Developing the ability to speak for yourself is an important step in the process of gaining respect and assurance. You should make it perfectly clear that the opinions, thoughts, and preferences you express belong to you and you alone. Have the courage to take full responsibility for your words. Claim sole possession of your intentions and feelings.

### *You Can't Know Something About Everything!*

You will always face situations where someone has more knowledge or expertise in a particular area than you do. Many women feel inferior, because in their minds they don't measure up to a particular situation. They allow themselves to feel intimidated by the person they're talking to. Consequently, they lack the confidence to assert themselves when appropriate.

Look at it this way. Everyone is uninformed about something. It may be about medical problems, wines, geography, cooking, football, fixing a roof, or buying tires! It's just that we're all uninformed about different things. It just isn't possible for anyone to know something about everything! Will Rogers once said, "We're all ignorant about something—just different subjects."

Your ability to communicate assertively should not be dependent on how much you know or don't know. It should be based on how you feel about yourself. Never feel inadequate when you lack information. Don't feel intimidated when the other person knows more than you do. You can lack information and still feel confident. Don't undermine yourself. Don't make comments by which you disavow your remarks. Show you validate your own convictions, feelings, and behavior. Have the courage and confidence to say, "I don't know," "I need advice," "I need more information," or "I want another opinion so I can make an informed decision." Remember, you can't know something about everything. No one does.

### Use "I" Language

Many women find it difficult to use the pronoun "I" when speaking. They feel others may not approve of or like them for making such clear, direct, statements. Women have often been socialized to believe that saying "I" or "I want" is selfish or self-centered.

Those close to you are not mind readers. The only way people are going to know what your feelings are is if you tell them. It's time to say what you want when you want to say it. After all, when a cat's tail is accidentally stepped on, the cat meows. When you bump your elbow on a hard surface, you cry out too. Well, it's time to lose your inhibitions about speaking up for yourself. Give yourself the credit for your thoughts and feelings by making a conscious effort to use the pronoun "I" regularly.

Notice how the following statements can be expressed using "I" language:

| Observation | Direct "I" Language Statement |
|---|---|
| Let's lower our voices, shall we? | I'd like you to lower your voice, please. |
| You shouldn't contradict me. | I'd appreciate your not contradicting me. |
| Mrs. L. is uncooperative. | I find Mrs. L to be uncooperative. |
| It may be best to start over. | I recommend that we start over. |

"I" language is self-assertive language. It expresses your own opinion or perception and doesn't directly attack anything the other party has done or said. On the other hand, "you" language can be aggressive. "You" statements, such as "You should have," "You always," or "You never" sound like accusations and make people defensive.

Consider the difference between "you" language and "I" language in the following examples:

| Aggressive "You" Language | Assertive "I" Language |
|---|---|
| You're wrong. | I disagree with you. |
| You never call on me at meetings. | I want you to call on me at meetings. |
| You always take credit for my ideas. | I'd like to receive credit for my ideas. |

Dr. Robert Bramson, author of *Coping With Difficult People,* writes, "By using ["I" language phrases], you have not told the other person what to do, how to feel or think, or even that he or she is wrong. You are instead signaling that you are expressing your own views or perceptions."

Women frequently use a passive grammatical style of speaking to avoid direct communication. By using the passive voice, they avoid responsibility for their behavior. Allow your grammar to reveal your successes as well as mistakes.

Observe how the passive voice may be converted into direct "I" language.

| *Passive* | *Active "I" Language* |
|---|---|
| No receipt was provided. | I did not receive a receipt. |
| The report was written to document employee productivity. | I wrote the report to document employment productivity. |
| The file was misplaced. | I misplaced the file. |
| A thorough job was done. | I did a thorough job. |

Now that you have the idea, practice making such "I" language comments as *I, I want, I don't want, I like, I feel, I need, I agree, I disagree* to express your feelings. Practice making such "I" language statements as *I wrote it, I accomplished it, I recommend it, I did it* to take credit for your efforts.

Another strategy many women use to avoid direct assertions is to beat around the bush or hint at what they want by phrasing their preference as questions.

*Example:* You enter your teenager's room and ask, "Don't you think the music is a bit loud?" You really mean, "*I'd* like you to please lower the volume."

*Example:* You have an idea to propose to your supervisor and ask, "Do you think it would be a good idea to hire extra personnel during peak hours of operation?" You really want to assert, "*I* recommend that we hire extra personnel to assist during peak hours of operation."

*Example:* You don't like the location of the table to which you've been shown in a restaurant. You ask, "Isn't this table stuck away in the corner?" You really mean, "*I'd* prefer a more centrally located table please."

*Example:* Having been at a party for hours, you're tired. You want to go home desperately. You turn to your companion and ask, "Are you ready to leave yet?" You really mean, *"I'm* exhausted; *I'd* like to leave now."

In an article she wrote for the *Washington Post,* Deborah Tannen,, Ph.D., presents a perfect example illustrating the tendency women have to indirectly express their wishes as questions. A couple were having a conversation while riding in their car. The wife asked, "Would you like to stop for a drink?" Her husband answered, "No," and they didn't stop. He was later frustrated to learn that his wife was annoyed because she had wanted to stop for a drink. He wondered, "Why didn't she just say what she wanted? Why did she play games with me?"

As you can see, phrasing your requests as questions often leads to confusion and misunderstanding. Others will take your needs and wants much more seriously if you phrase them as assertive "I" language statements.

Take advantage of every opportunity to use "I" language. Keep track of the number of times you are able to use the pronoun "I" to express your opinions, feelings, and achievements. And don't worry, it will not make you appear selfish or egotistical. It will help you sound confident, natural, and direct.

Remember my friend Marla and her fictitious husband? *She* was too timid to let the auto repair shop manager know that *she* was the one who wanted a written estimate. *She* was the one who felt his price was too high. *She* was the one who wanted to comparison shop before making a decision. Her insecurity about the value of her own opinions caused her to credit another person with them. Marla was single, yet she invented a make-believe mate to give more credibility to her own judgment. This habit of indirectly stating her true feelings by attributing them to someone else only serves to further erode her self-esteem. She needs to be direct and speak for herself. She will get the same results and feel a lot better about herself in the process. A direct "I" language response that would have indicated Marla is responsible for her own words would be:

"*I* will not make a decision without a written estimate. Please provide one. Your price seems a bit high even with the discount. *I* need to get a couple of other estimates before *I* proceed. If yours is the best, *I'll* be back. Thanks for your time."

Lara, a college professor, reacted in a similar fashion. Paul, an academic advisor, interrupted Lara's class to request she allow a student to register late and be admitted. Lara stated the student had already missed the first two weeks. She suggested the student wait until the beginning of a new term to enroll. Paul persisted and asked her to make an exception. Flustered, Lara hedged, "My department chairman told us [the teaching faculty] not to admit new students after the first week of classes. He said it is impossible to make up all the missed work. So, I'll have to talk to him to see if I can make an exception."

Lara was a tenured professor with years of experience. Nevertheless, she lacked the self-confidence needed to assert her decision directly. She used her department chairman as the excuse not to enroll the student. In reality, she had the authority to make the decision. Lara needed a personal verbal fitness trainer. She was annoyed with herself for her fearfulness. She asked my advice about how to respond if a similar situation ever presented itself. I encouraged her not to reproach herself for her previous timidity. I assured her she would have plenty of future opportunities to be assertive. It wasn't a matter of "if" but of "when." I suggested she mentally prepare herself to be ready with a firm, assertive "I" language response.

"Excuse me, Paul, I'm in the middle of a class. But just so you know, I will not allow any student to enroll in my course two weeks after it begins unless there are extraordinary circumstances. I'll be pleased to discuss this with you later."

Of course, assertive "I" language communication won't always get you what you want or guarantee that your wishes are respected. However, it does increase the odds in your favor. The advantage of using "I" language regularly is that regardless of the outcome, you maintain your self-respect and feel better about yourself.

Joanna, my friend's nineteen-year-old daughter, picked me up in her car for a lunch date. As she turned her car over to the parking valet at the restaurant, she said, "Please don't fool with the radio. This is my father's car. He gets really angry when he has to reset the radio to his favorite station."

Knowing the car was Joanna's and not her father's, I was surprised. I asked why she didn't simply say, "I prefer you to leave my radio set where it is," or "Please don't change my radio station." Joanna shrugged her shoulders. "They never pay attention to me anyway."

I introduced my philosophy about the importance of using "I" language. Joanna listened thoughtfully without commenting. After lunch, the valet brought the car. As we were driving away, Joanna noticed the radio station had been changed. She abruptly stopped the car and jumped out in search of the valet. I heard her chide, "I specifically asked you not to change the radio station in my car. Please tell me why you didn't honor my request." The parking attendant sheepishly replied, "Sorry, miss, it won't happen again." Joanna felt elated that she expressed her feelings and didn't ignore the situation by simply driving away.

So, make an effort to use "I" language frequently. You'll be amazed at your newfound sense of personal power and confidence.

## Typical Communication Styles

Before continuing to the exercises that follow, let's review the differences between the typical communication styles introduced in chapter 1. The timid/indirect style has been added to more specifically differentiate between the four common response types. You will quickly be able to recognize which styles you and people you know use on a regular basis.

| | |
|---|---|
| Submissive | I'm not important/You're important |
| Timid/indirect | I'm somewhat important but tend to be unsure of myself |
| Assertive | We're both important |
| Aggressive | I'm important/You're not important |

The *submissive* response is often no response at all. It demonstrates you put yourself last and consider yourself inferior to others. It indicates you are willing to surrender your own rights to fulfill the needs and desires of everyone else.

The *timid/indirect* response implies you lack faith in your own judgment. Although it demonstrates a tiny effort to stand up for yourself, it characterizes you as an individual lacking confidence or the strength of your convictions. It's a response which gives someone else the credit for your thoughts and feelings.

The *assertive* response reveals you have a healthy self-concept and expresses your opinions and ideas clearly and directly. It indicates you consider yourself equal to others and intend to make sure your wants and needs are respected while you respect the interests of others. The purpose of an assertive response is to show your intent to speak up for yourself and make your own choices. It permits you to escape the negative effects of submissive, indirect, or aggressive communication.

The *aggressive* response is somewhat belligerent and militant in nature and tends to be delivered in a loud, hostile voice. It shows you believe your opinions and feelings are all important and people must defer to your wishes. It demonstrates lack of regard for the rights of others. The purpose of an aggressive response is frequently to embarrass or insult rather than to directly convey honest feelings. Aggressive individuals try to get their way by intimidating others.

Shirley is a perfect example of the successful professional woman who becomes annoyed with herself when she responds to requests in a submissive or timid/indirect way. She is an occupational therapist with her own chain of hand rehabilitation clinics.

In one situation, Shirley quoted a patient her customary fee of $35 for ultrasound therapy. The patient asked her to accept $20. As Shirley feels extremely uncomfortable "bargaining" with patients, she submissively agreed to reduce the fee. She was later annoyed with herself for her lack of assertion, not to mention worried that her other patients would find out they were being charged more for the same service.

Realizing that reducing her fee for one patient was unfair to her other patients and not at all in her best interest professionally,

Shirley vowed to never again acquiesce in a similar situation. The next time a patient asked for a fee reduction, Shirley was a bit more prepared. She responded, "Oh, you'll have to take that up with my office manager. He's in charge of establishing and collecting fees for the professional services provided." Such a timid/indirect response left Shirley annoyed with herself once again. After all, she's the boss. She's the one who has the authority to make the decisions. I told her, "Shirley, *you're* in charge here. Stop passing the buck. It's time to practice assertive 'I' language communication!"

Together, Shirley and I brainstormed the perfect response for her to use in the future. Here's what we came up with: "My fees are not negotiable. If you're pressed financially, I'll be happy to work out a convenient payment plan for you. Otherwise, I invite you to call other therapists. I'm sure you'll find that my fees are customary and reasonable."

**EXERCISE**

Read the following scenarios. Pretend you are the woman involved in each of them. Take a moment to think of an assertive, "I" language response that demonstrates you are clearly taking credit for your words. The sample responses are included to help you contrast the differences between the four common communication styles.

*Situation:* In an electronics store, a young woman is considering the purchase of a VCR. The salesman has spent a lot of time with her explaining the myriad features (memory, remote control, programming capabilities, number of channels, etc.) of a particularly expensive model. The young woman listens politely to the whole sales pitch. Upon completion of his "spiel," the salesman asks, "How would you like to pay for it—cash, check, or credit card?" *How would you respond?*

*SAMPLE RESPONSES*

*Submissive:* The young woman, feeling obligated because the salesman spent so much time with her, responds, "I guess I'll pay with my credit card." Although she's not sure she wants that particular model, she purchases it. Arriving home, feeling guilty for having spent so much money on a VCR with features she doesn't need, she gets a friend to accompany her back to the store to return it for a refund.

*Timid/indirect:* The young women responds, "My husband said I shouldn't spend more than $200 for a VCR. He said if it is more than that it probably has a lot of features we'll never use."

*Aggressive:* The young woman responds, "How dare you waste my time showing me something in which I have no interest? How dare you presume I'm ready to buy anything from you? You have some nerve. I tried to tell you what I wanted but you wouldn't listen. I have no intention of ever buying anything from you."

*Assertive:* The young woman responds, "Frankly, I'm not ready to purchase anything. I don't object to your wanting to make a sale, but I'm not interested in that particular VCR. It has too many features I'll never use. How about a more basic model? Please show me something in the range of $200 or less."

*Situation:* A woman is irritated when a realtor directs all his remarks to her husband and repeatedly refers to her as "the little lady." *How would you respond?*

### Sample Responses

*Submissive:* She says nothing, silently vowing not to buy a house from this realtor under any circumstances. She asks no questions and tunes him out completely.

*Timid/indirect:* Waiting until the realtor is out of earshot, she turns to her husband, whispering, "Would you please tell him to stop calling me 'the little lady.' It's driving me up a wall."

*Aggressive:* She screams at the realtor, "Stop calling me little lady, you obnoxious, condescending chauvinist. I wouldn't buy a house from you if you were the last realtor in town!"

*Assertive:* Looking directly at the realtor, she says, "Excuse me, I'm sure you don't mean to be condescending, but I'm as much involved in the decision to buy a new home as my husband. Please stop referring to me as 'the little lady.' My name is Mrs. Howell."

*Situation:* A college student living on campus is being pressured by her other two roommates to share an off-campus apartment with them. They want to be in the new apartment in time for the start of the new semester. The student really prefers living in the dormitory for a variety of reasons. However, she is concerned they'll resent her if she causes the threesome to split up by refusing their request. *How would you respond?*

### SAMPLE RESPONSES

*Submissive:* The student, against her better judgment, agrees to move into an apartment with her friends. She keeps hoping her roommates will change their mind but they don't. She is unhappy with her decision and is so nervous and upset for the rest of the semester that her grades suffer.

*Timid/indirect:* The student asks her father to be the "heavy" and tell her friends he won't let her move off campus. She later laments, "I'm really annoyed with my dad but there is nothing I can do about it. He won't change his mind."

*Aggressive:* The student responds, "I don't want to move off campus. You knew that when we agreed to be roommates. You two have no sense of loyalty. So go ahead, move into your apartment and break up the friendship."

*Assertive:* The student tells her roommates, "Thanks for inviting me to join you, but I prefer living in the dorm. I feel safer here and I don't want the responsibility and expense of an apartment. I'll miss you both if you decide to leave, but I'll understand. Let's all try to remain good friends."

*Situation:* After determining a young man's wisdom teeth were impacted, an oral surgeon recommended to his mother that all four teeth be removed at the same time. As he had a cancellation the following day, he urged her to take advantage of the immediate opportunity for him to perform the surgery. If she didn't, her son would have to wait at least six weeks for the next available appointment and might experience discomfort. The woman really wants a second opinion and a chance to talk to several friends whose children have gone through oral surgery. *How would you respond?*

*Submissive:* Intimidated by the doctor's brusque authoritative style, the mother asks no questions and makes the appointment for the following day.

*Timid/indirect:* The woman books the appointment but, upon arriving home, asks her husband to call the doctor's office and cancel it. He provides the excuse that she had forgotten about a previous commitment and would reschedule at a later date.

*Aggressive:* The mother responds, "You have some nerve. You just want to fill the canceled slot as quickly as possible. You don't have my son's best interests at heart. Well, doctor, you can't pull that on me."

*Assertive:* The mother responds, "I appreciate your recommendation. First I have several questions." After receiving the responses, she says, "Thank you for your time and information. We cannot make such a snap decision and need to discuss it further."

Okay, how did you do? How did your responses compare with the sample ones? If you've been following my advice in this book your reactions will be similar to the Assertive choice of each situation. As you can see, this preferred response style shows how the women involved used polite and direct, no nonsense "I" language to speak for themselves.

In all fairness, it isn't always women who take the timid/indirect approach when communicating and avoid speaking for themselves. You might be familiar with "The Courtship of Miles Standish," a poem written in the 1800s by Henry Wadsworth Longfellow. In it, Miles Standish, a widower and the Puritan Captain of Plymouth, wanted to marry the lovely Priscilla. Too timid to speak to her himself, he begged his dear friend, John Alden, to approach her on his behalf. When John Alden tried to refuse the request, Miles Standish said:

> *I am a maker of war, not a maker of phrases,*
> *You, who are bred as a scholar, can say it in elegant language.*
> *Such as you read in your books of the pleadings and wooings of*
> *   lovers,*
> *Such as you think best adapted to win the heart of a maiden.*

John Alden, although secretly in love with Priscilla himself, could not refuse to do his loyal friend this favor. With a very heavy heart, he tried to eloquently convince Priscilla to become his friend's wife. Longfellow writes:

> *But as he warmed and glowed, in his simple and eloquent language.*
> *Quite forgetful of self, and full of the praise of his rival,*
> *Archly the maiden smiled, and, with eyes overrunning with laughter,*
> *Said in a tremulous voice, "Why don't you speak for yourself, John?"*

## You Are the One Behind the Message

You can do it too! Get into the habit of speaking for yourself and taking the credit for what you say. You will be amazed by the aura of self-confidence you radiate. Your self-assured manner and composure will speak for itself. It will tell the listener that you are secure with your decision *and* you mean it!

Remember, your beliefs are as important and worthy as anyone else's. Whether the perfect response is a simple "No" or "That's not acceptable," it should be *you* delivering the words, not your boyfriend, father, son, or make-believe mate! If you choose not to buy a product pitched by a telemarketer, say so yourself. Leave your husband out of the conversation. Make every effort to use "I" language frequently. Use it to express feelings and take personal responsibility for your actions. Chapter 9, "Speak Up on the Job," deals with the importance of using "I" language and taking credit for your accomplishments in a business environment.

Speaking for yourself will identify you as the person behind the message. If you don't take verbal responsibility and credit for what you say, you deny your self-worth. There should never be a question in the listener's mind that the comments and ideas you assert are yours rather than someone else's. If you are confident and secure when you speak, people will listen and show you respect. You will gain courage and confidence by speaking for yourself.

So, make an effort to use "I" language frequently. You'll be amazed at your newfound sense of personal power and confidence.

# 8

# *Don't Put Up With Put-Downs*

Vickie, an assistant principal, was the only woman on a school district's administrative team. Whenever she made a suggestion, Marc, the principal of another school, rolled his eyes and sarcastically announced, "Everyone listen, Gracie has something to say," (referring to Gracie Allen, the wife of George Burns). Annoyed by Marc's persistent efforts to devalue her ideas, Vickie finally decided to stand up for herself. She was careful to keep her composure and playfully quipped, "Excuse me, George, if you don't have anything to contribute, why don't you go sit in the corner and smoke a cigar?" Marc responded, "Touché," and allowed Vicky to continue without further interruption. When Marc later saw Vicky in the faculty lounge, he commented with admiration, "I wondered how much longer you were going to let me keep calling you Gracie!" He subsequently treated Vicky with esteem and deference.

## *Bullies May Become Buddies*

The "stand up to the bully and he'll become your buddy" phenomenon has been demonstrated time and time again. Verbal abusers don't try to intimidate, make unreasonable demands, or act disrespectful to those people they can't manipulate or put down.

Psychologists explain that this is because the bullies admire individuals they view as strong. They expect you to be as submissive as their other victims and will test you to see how much abuse you'll accept. In a peculiar way, these difficult types only respect people who let them know, "You're out of line. You can't say that to me." It wasn't until Vicky stood up to Marc that he viewed her as being worthy of respect.

I love to tell the story of the waitress who was on her break when her boss screamed at her for some minor mistake she made earlier in the day. She stood up, looked him straight in the eye, and said, "Never speak to me like that again." She told me he apologized, promoted her to maitre d' within a year, and treated her respectfully until she stopped working for him five years later.

### What Motivates Verbal Bullies?

When my son Jeremy was four years old, he came home from preschool crying. "Colleen said 'stupid head' to me," he wailed. "Why do people say ugly things to each other for no reason, Mommy?" I didn't have a good answer for him then, but thanks to former Notre Dame University football coach Lou Holtz and a plethora of psychology books, I have one now.

Lou Holtz was a featured speaker at an Anthony Robbins/Peter Lowe Success Seminar at the Miami Arena. He told over 25,000 people that he used to insult his wife and criticize her every chance he got. During lunch, I had the opportunity to personally ask him why. He told me, "Because I had very low self-esteem. I wanted to make my wife feel worthless too, so she'd be grateful to be with a guy like me." I thanked him for his candid response and thought to myself, Wow! It takes a brave man to admit something like that to himself, let alone to strangers.

People say mean, insensitive, and rude things for many reasons. Verbal abusers often have very little self-esteem and don't feel good about themselves. Because they are unhappy, they put you down to make you unhappy too. By making you feel worse, they feel better. As the saying goes, "Misery loves company." Other individuals have a need to dominate and control. They insult you for the feelings of power and superiority it gives them. After all, if belittling or insulting remarks didn't satisfy some need, no one would make them. Some cut-you-downers say nasty things because they're jealous, they've had a bad day, or someone was nasty to them.

I firmly believe that most people don't make belittling remarks because they're miserable, malevolent, or jealous. Instead, they're just insensitive and unaware of others' feelings. They say stupid things without meaning to. These oblivious souls are clueless and simply lack the social grace to know what *not* to say in a particular situation. As discussed in chapter 1, "Be Unappealing to Users and Abusers," politely pointing out insulting comments might be all that is needed to start verbal bullies on the road to reform. Bullies often apologize and change when made aware of their behavior. And if they don't change, it's probably time to "unplug" from them.

### Put-Downs Come in All Sizes and Shapes

Unfortunately, the world abounds with people who insult or verbally abuse others for the reasons previously discussed. Our language provides such difficult people with countless ways to put others down. They can use it to attack you directly, ask sarcastic questions, or make condescending or patronizing remarks.

Put-downs may be direct or indirect. *Direct put-downs* are easy to recognize. They are delivered aggressively as undisguised insults. "You are really stupid," "A moron could have done a better job," or "You are the laziest, most irresponsible person I've ever met" are examples of verbally direct put-downs.

*Group put-downs* are a type of direct put-down. They target or pigeonhole you as being inferior for belonging to a particular group or minority. Such groups might include women, Jews, African Americans, the mentally retarded, the physically disabled, the elderly, and so forth. "Dumb blonde" jokes, ethnic jokes, or such comments as "What do you know? You're a woman," or "I'm surprised you don't drink more, being Irish and all" are examples of group put-downs.

*Indirect put-downs* include sarcastic, condescending, and patronizing remarks or questions. These put-downs aren't always easy ᴵⁿ ᵣₑcᵒᵍⁿⁱₛₑ because they are indirect and may be disguised as compliments. They verbal abuser's clever use of innuendo and subtle digs makes the put-down harder to figure out. Examples of backhanded compliments are, "Your haircut looks nice. It doesn't make your nose look too big," or as Rowina said to her husband's ex-wife (Bette Midler) in the movie *That Old Feeling*, "Congratulations! You look much better than the last time I saw you." Other examples are, "That color would really look great on you if you were ten years younger," "This recipe would work even better with good quality meat," or "Has your social life improved yet?"

*Nonverbal put-downs* are the least obvious of all because nothing is actually said aloud. Instead of using words to put you down, some bullies creatively use facial expressions, mannerisms, and gestures to belittle you or your ideas. They might ignore you in a conversation or address everything they say to your spouse, for example. Rolling eyes upward toward the heavens, shaking a head negatively from side to side, a thumbs-down signal, a fist being shaken at you, an exasperated sigh, excessively loud yawning, or continuously staring off into space while you're speaking are other examples of nonverbal put-downs.

### EXERCISE

Think of some examples of put-downs or snide remarks you have received or have heard directed to someone else. Try to think of one for each category and write them down. You'll need them to complete exercises later in the chapter.

### DIRECT PUT-DOWNS

*Example:* "How could you be so dumb as to forget your wallet?"
*Your Example:*

### GROUP PUT-DOWNS

*Example:* Q: "What do you call five blondes sitting in a circle?" A: "A dope ring."
*Your Example:*

## INDIRECT PUT-DOWNS

*Example:* "You're brave to be showing off those legs."
*Your Example:*


## NONVERBAL PUT-DOWNS

*Example:* My friend's boss blatantly refused to acknowledge her
when she raised her hand to speak at a meeting.
*Your Example:*


### You Owe It to Yourself to Respond

Regardless of a verbal bully's motivation for insulting you, or the
nature of the put-down, you owe it to yourself to stand up to that
individual. If you don't, you deny yourself as a person. You will feel
overrun and helpless with a diminished sense of self-worth.

In his classic book *Coping With Difficult People,* Dr. Robert M.
Bramson advises that the first rule of coping with verbal bullies is
to stand up to them. If you let them push you around, they'll never
see you as someone worthy of attention. Dr. Bramson writes, "Your
acquiescence will be taken not simply as a sign that you're not
worth bothering about but as a license to squash you. In coping
with these very Difficult People, it helps to recognize that the fear
and confusion you feel are natural, even appropriate, reactions to
being attacked. Expect to feel distracted, angry or awkward, but say
something of a standing up nature anyway."

People who get put down allow themselves to be put down and
are just as responsible as the put-down artists. Your self-esteem
depends upon your ability to recognize and neutralize a verbal
abusers' wisecracks. If you interpret someone's comments as a put-
down, you owe it to your yourself to respond assertively.
Otherwise, the anger or humiliation you feel will gnaw at you and
fester until you do respond.

The purpose of your response isn't to change the difficult
person, although it might do just that! The purpose of your
response is to say something that makes you feel better about

yourself. Your goal is to deflect the insult and not allow it to succeed in hitting its mark—you! A polite assertive response, free of anger and hostility, will help you to accomplish your goal.

You're probably thinking, "But I never know what to say," "Her insult came out of nowhere and took me by surprise," or "I always think of a great comeback hours later." Of course, it's impossible to know exactly when and where you'll be the recipient of an insulting or hurtful remark. However, with a bit of advance planning, you can be ready. The best preparation is to be familiar with different methods for deflecting unfair criticism and hurtful remarks. Learn and practice the techniques described on the following pages. You'll soon find yourself able to consistently think of effective on-the-spot responses to verbal attacks. Be sure to accompany your response with assertive body language. Remember, eye contact communicates courage. It helps you feel and look confident even when you're not. So whether you use the genuine inquiry method, agree with the criticism, state your position, use humor, or trade "a quip for a quip," look critics in the eye. Let them know that they can't intimidate you or erode your self-esteem.

### *"What Do You Mean by That?"*

My family and I were having dinner in a restaurant. I asked the waitress to please bring us spoons for our coffee. After she did, I noticed we had no cream or sugar either. Calling her back to the table, I politely brought the oversight to her attention. Sighing impatiently, she rolled her eyes and muttered, "Oh, for heaven's sake!" The waitress's attitude bothered me. I couldn't be sure whether she was simply having a bad day or if she was annoyed by my requests. I decided to clarify the situation by asking her directly, "What did you mean by that? Are you annoyed by my requests?" She immediately replied, "No! I'm annoyed with myself for being so forgetful. I'll be right back with your cream and sugar."

Asking for clarification or genuine inquire has several advantages when you interpret someone's remark as an insult. It clarifies whether the speaker intended to belittle you. It frequently wards off the feelings of resentment that come between people due to a misunderstanding. Even if the cut-you-downer meant the remark as a dig and plays innocent by denying it, that's fine. You've exposed that person, protected your self-esteem, and given him or her a way to save face.

After the waitress responded so impolitely, I needed to clarify the situation for my own personal satisfaction. By asking her, "What did you mean by that?" I brought the problem out in the open. Whether or not she was telling the truth about being annoyed with herself or just trying to save face isn't important. Had I not dealt with the incident directly, I would have harbored feelings of ill will toward that waitress and perhaps never returned to the restaurant. That would have been a shame because their food is great!

Asking for clarification or genuine inquiry works best when you are faced with indirect or nonverbal put-downs. Whenever you suspect a person's intent is to discount you, ask them for clarification. Try using such questions as:

What did you mean by that?
I'm not sure what you meant. Would you please explain?
That sounded like a put-down, was it?
It sounds like you're insulting me, are you?
Why did you roll your eyes while I was talking?
Your body language makes me think you don't agree with me.
    Am I correct?

Remember the story about Anne and Peggy? Anne used the "ask for clarification/genuine inquiry" technique very effectively. Peggy had requested that UPS leave a package at Anne's house. When Anne later gave Peggy her parcel, Peggy exclaimed, "I'm sure glad you didn't know what was in the box. Those are the diamond earrings my daughter sent." Anne immediately assumed that Peggy was questioning her honesty. Fortunately, Anne asked for clarification, "Why are you glad I didn't know what was in the box?" Peggy replied, "Because had you known, you might have been unwilling to accept such a valuable package."

Anne's genuine inquiry probably saved the friendship. It helped her avoid feeling resentful toward Peggy for a misinterpreted remark.

Requesting clarification has another advantage. It sends the put-down right back where it came from. Verbal bullies often hide behind the indirect innuendo or backhanded compliment. By having the wisecrack boomerang on them, it becomes their job, not yours, to deal with it. Once they realize that you have the courage to bring their put-downs out into the open, their sails lose wind.

Asking for clarification/genuine inquiry would also have worked for Vicky. In response to Marc's sarcastic announcement, "Everyone listen, Gracie has something to say," Vicky could have inquired, "What do you mean by that?" or "I don't understand."

Obviously, Marc's comment implied that Vicky was a scatterbrained airhead like Gracie's TV personality. However, Marc probably would have been too embarrassed to specifically explain that in front of the others. Of course, Vicky's quip, "Excuse me, George, if you don't have anything to contribute, why don't you go sit in a corner and smoke a cigar?" was certainly effective. I just want to illustrate that one or all of the methods for deflecting put-downs might work in any given situation

Asking for clarification helps us in several ways. It allows us to clarify perceived criticism in order to avoid unnecessary misunderstandings. It also brings negative intent out into the open where it can be dealt with directly.

### EXERCISE

Use the put-downs or negative criticisms you identified on page 129. Think about how you might use the "genuine inquiry" technique in response to at least two of them.

*EXAMPLE*

*Put-Down:* My friend was dating a man several years younger than herself. I overheard a coworker snidely comment, "I hear you're robbing the cradle."

*Possible "Genuine Inquiry" Responses:*
   1. Whatever do you mean by that?
   2. That sounded like a snide remark. Did you mean it that way?

### *"You're Right"*

Iris was about to have several cavities filled. She asked her dentist to apply topical anesthesia to her gums in order to deaden the discomfort of the novocaine injection. He snidely remarked, "Boy, are you ever a wimp!" Iris was annoyed with his attitude but didn't allow herself to become defensive. Instead, she good-naturedly agreed, "You bet I'm a wimp! Now please anesthetize my gums before giving me the shot of novocaine."

Saying "You're right!" is a great way to empower yourself to cast off remarks meant to discount you. By agreeing with the criticism, you can prevent damage to your self-esteem and show that you are confident and secure.

Iris used this technique beautifully. She didn't try to justify herself or get defensive. She simply agreed with the dentist and repeated her request. In essence, she was saying, "Yep, I'm a wimp. So what? Now, do what I asked!" Once critics realize you are not bothered by the criticism, criticizing you stops being fun for them.

It's often effective to agree with only part of a criticism. Agree with the part that directly states an observation and ignore the part that is indirectly meant to belittle you.

For example, my friend Meryl is a lawyer for a large Miami law firm. She was invited to conduct a seminar at a legal conference in Orlando. Gary, a local attorney, met her at the airport. He greeted her sarcastically, "You must be the crackerjack lady lawyer from Miami who thinks she knows more than we do." Meryl pleasantly asserted, "Well, I am the crackerjack lady lawyer from Miami."

Meryl agreed with the objective information in Gary's snide remark—her sex, her profession, and her hometown. She deftly ignored his sarcastic implication that she considered herself to be better and brighter than lawyers in Orlando. She didn't allow Gary to goad her into a defensive or hostile response. Meryl effectively neutralized what promised to be an unpleasant verbal conflict.

Alice entertains herself by criticizing coworkers. She enjoys upsetting others and putting them on the defensive. Walking into Rena's office, she was true to form. "Rena, your office is a disaster. You have boxes and papers all over the place. I don't know how you can stand working in such a mess. You're so disorganized." Alice was implying that Rena was sloppy and disorganized. Rena played right into her hands by becoming defensive. "Oh, I'm not always this messy. It's just that I've been so busy. I haven't had time to organize the boxes because I'm working on a new project, and the new file cabinets haven't arrived so I can't file all the papers." It's precisely this type of defensive response that entertains, even empowers, verbal bullies like Alice and encourages their put-downs.

Rena could have neutralized the negative implication by simply agreeing with part of Alice's criticism. "Yes, Alice, I certainly do have boxes and papers all over the place." Such a direct assertive response would have deprived Alice of the perverse satisfaction she receives when her victims become defensive. Alice would be discouraged from making future attacks.

Once you're comfortable with the "agree" technique, try adding a remark of your own. This will further confirm that you are secure and at ease with your own thoughts, opinions, and behaviors. Verbal abusers will soon realize that snide remarks are unlikely to pierce your armor of confidence. Putting you down will cease to be fun. They'll have to go elsewhere for their entertainment!

The following anecdotes show how the technique worked for me.

My first book, an English pronunciation drill book, had just been published. Mel, another professor in my field, caught up to me as I was walking across campus. He had a copy of my book in his hand. "Congratulations, Paulette. This is a nice book. It's really quite simplistic. I could have written it myself," he stated smugly. Well, that was a backhanded compliment if I ever heard one! "Yes, Mel, I'm sure you could have," I agreed charitably. "But you didn't, did you?" I added.

This technique was also effective in another situation. I had reapplied for a prestigious award for excellence in teaching that I had previously received at my college. A jealous colleague who had unsuccessfully applied for it several years in a row stated gleefully, "I hear you didn't get an Endowed Teaching Chair this year." "No Grant, I didn't," I agreed smiling. "But I'm sure those who did receive it deserve the honor," I added sincerely. Grant walked away expressing a "sour grapes" attitude, saying, "It's not that big a deal anyway."

Grant was extremely disappointed that he was passed over again for the award. He had hoped to make himself feel better by rubbing salt in my wounds. However, I wasn't wounded. Furthermore, I was truly pleased for this year's recipients of the honor. By simply agreeing with the accuracy of his remark, and adding a gracious one of my own, I neutralized his toxic intent.

Now take a look at how Iris, Meryl, and Rena could have added remarks of their own after using the "agree" technique.

Dentist: Boy, are you ever a wimp!
Iris: You bet I'm a wimp. And I come from a long line of wimps.

Gary: You must be the crackerjack lady lawyer from Miami who thinks she knows more than we do.
Meryl: Well, I am the crackerjack lady lawyer from Miami. And it's very nice to meet you!

Alice: Rena, your office is a disaster. You have boxes and papers all over the place. I don't know how you can stand working in such a mess. You're so disorganized.
Rena: Yes, Alice, I certainly do have boxes and papers all over the place. Was there something you wanted to tell me?

Assertively agreeing with your would-be detractors and making a remark of your own really takes the wind out of their sails. It will make them rethink their behavior and discourage them from making snide remarks to you in the future.

Many women mention they are often subjected to having their noses rubbed in their mistakes. They report that the criticism they hear most frequently is: "That was really dumb," or "That was pretty stupid." The "agree and add a remark of your own" technique works particularly well with this prevalent form of put-down behavior.

When I ran out of gas on I-93, the emergency roadside assistance representative arrived an hour later. He condescendingly said, "Lady, I gotta tell ya, forgetting to fill up your tank is really stupid." Having already berated myself for my forgetfulness, I didn't appreciate someone else adding insult to injury. I knew I had to respond or I'd feel even worse. "I agree. Forgetting to fill up my tank is really stupid. But your job is to help people, not dwell on their mistakes," I asserted.

The next time a critic delights in telling you how dumb it was to lose your keys, run out of gas, or forget where you parked, agree with him or her and add a remark of your own. Such responses as "It's not the first dumb thing I've ever done, not will it be the last," "Let he who has never done something stupid cast the first stone," or "You're right. That was one of the dumbest mistakes I've ever made. I'll be more careful in the future" are equally effective. The point is to show detractors that you are comfortable with who you are and that they can't rattle your emotional cage. This will neutralize critics' toxicity and prevent you from becoming a victim of belittling remarks.

Agreeing with your critics right to express an opinion is also an effective way to deflect negative criticism. Acknowledging your critic's opinion doesn't mean you agree with it. It simply means you're acknowledging his or her right to express it. This technique is particularly effective when you are the target of a direct put-down. Comments like, "You are certainly entitled to your opinion," "That's your opinion and you're certainly welcome to it," "I guess it looks that way to you," or "I'm sure you think so" work well. Be sure to avoid responses that smack of defensiveness. Examples:

*Put-Down:* Women over forty look ridiculous with long hair. You should cut yours.

*Defensive Response:* But people say I look young for my age. I didn't think my hair was that long, anyway.

*Assertive Response:* That's your opinion and you're certainly entitled to it!

*Put-Down:* You're always out of town on business. You can't
be a very good mother.

*Defensive Response:* I'm not really gone that much—only one
weekend a month. And I try to spend a lot of quality time
with my children every chance I get.

*Assertive Response:* I suppose it appears that way to you.

Openly thanking critics for negative but accurate observations is
another assertive technique. If a friend or acquaintance "innocently"
observes, "Gee, you've really gained a lot of weight," or "Your hair is
so gray," look her in the eye and agree. Then express your
appreciation for the remark. Try saying, "Yes, I have gained weight.
Thanks for mentioning it in front of my friends," or "Yes, my hair has
gotten quite gray. Thank you for bringing it to my attention." This
will give her pause and cause her to rethink her behavior.

Remember, never apologize for being you. Don't rise to take the
critic's bait and respond defensively. Avoid lengthy explanations
and stifle any impulse to justify your beliefs or behavior. By
agreeing with your critics, acknowledging their opinions, or even
thanking them, you may discourage them from taking future
potshots at you. More important than that, you'll feel great about
yourself.

**EXERCISE**

Use the put-downs or negative criticisms you identified on page
129. Think about how you might use the "agree" technique in
response to at least two of them.

*EXAMPLE*

*Put-Down:* You forgot to put money in your checking account
and bounced three checks. Your friend says, "That was
really dumb to be so forgetful."

*Possible "Agree" Responses:*
1. "Yes, thanks for confirming what I already know. I'd better
be more careful in the future or it'll happen again."
2. "You're absolutely right. And we all make mistakes!"

## Humor Works

I was in a crowded elevator in a downtown office building. A woman accidentally leaned against the panel of buttons causing the elevator to stop on every floor. An irate passenger aggressively barked, "That was really moronic." Unflustered, the woman apologized to everyone and joked, "I usually do one moronic thing a day. I'm sure glad I've got that one behind me!" The other passengers chuckled and shrugged off the inconvenience of the extra stops. I thought the woman handled the situation beautifully. In fact, I seized the first opportunity I had to jot down her humorous comeback so I wouldn't forget it.

Using humor is a great way to neutralize put-downs. There will always be critical, judgmental people who try to anger or discount you. You don't have to let them. Humor counterbalances toxic comments and defuses verbal conflicts. It's a way to assert yourself and reduce the tension created by your critic's inappropriate or negative comments.

I used the humor technique to defuse a nasty comment about my work. At lunch with several coworkers, my friend began to describe this book, which I was writing at the time. When she explained that it dealt with assertive communication for women, Gil sarcastically announced, "Oh, just what the world needs, another Bitch Manual!" Everyone fell silent, anxious to see how I intended to "defend" my project. I decided not to play into his hands and become defensive about my purpose in writing *"Did You Say Something, Susan?"* Wanting to release the tension and keep the conversation friendly, I humorously replied, "Congratulations and thank you for that remark, Gil. It's exactly what I needed to make a point. You just earned yourself a spot in my book!" Everyone laughed and was relieved I didn't dampen the pleasant mood by becoming indignant at Gil's obvious dig.

Allow yourself to be amused rather than antagonized by a put-down artist's barbs. Make a humorous or entertaining comment if you can. Your goal is to stand up for yourself and show the verbal bully that his or her remarks can't shake your confidence.

After lightening my hair several years ago, I found myself the target of the then popular "dumb blonde" jokes. Whenever I indicated my displeasure at such jokes, others present would come to the so-called comedian's defense, accusing me of not having a sense of humor. "Where's your sense of humor?" or "You're too sensitive. Stop taking the jokes personally," they'd say. I realized I needed a response that would allow me to defuse their criticism and stand up for myself at the same time. Finally, thanks to an anecdote I read in a magazine about how Dolly Parton handled herself in the same situation, I had the perfect rejoinder. The next time the "friend of a friend" accused me of taking his jokes too personally, I was ready. "Whatever gave you the idea I took your jokes personally? Number one: I'm not dumb. And, number two. I'm not really blonde!" After everyone had a hearty laugh, I continued, "Seriously, Jack, I find such jokes to be offensive. Please purge them from your repertoire when I'm around." The jokester actually mumbled an apology and never subjected me to his toxic humor again.

Even U.S. presidents have used the humor technique to deflect criticism. President Ronald Reagan was really skilled at this. When snide remarks were made about his falling asleep in cabinet meetings, he said, "With so many trouble spots around the world, I've told my aides that if they hear of any trouble they should wake me up immediately, even when I'm in a cabinet meeting."

Some of you might be thinking, "But I'm not clever like that. I'm not good at thinking up humorous comebacks instantly." Don't despair! Most people, even professional entertainers and comedians, aren't either. All those witty remarks that great teachers, speakers, comics, and talk show hosts come up with are usually prepared and rehearsed, not spur of the moment ad libs.

Take some time to read through some of the many joke books that have funny comebacks to rude remarks. Memorize a few so you'll have them to use on the spur of the moment. Stay alert for humorous remarks used by others. When you hear a comedian or talk show host on TV make a particularly witty remark, write it down. If you're reading a newspaper or magazine and a joke catches your eye, remember it. When I read about Dolly Parton's clever comeback to "dumb blonde" jokes, I memorized it. Sure enough, I used it to my benefit on the perfect occasion. And everyone thought I was so witty to think of such a clever response off the top of my head!

Here are some examples of humorous responses I've heard used to defuse commonly heard put-downs. They've become part of my collection. You might want to add several of them to yours. Remember, your goal is to relieve tension and show you're not bothered by the criticism. Be sure to avoid becoming defensive. Responding with sarcasm or hostility makes everyone uncomfortable, including any observers. So, when the appropriate occasion presents itself, deliver your lines in a good-natured or playful way.

*Put-Down:* That was really stupid.
*Response:* We all learn from our mistakes. And I've learned that I make lots of mistakes.

*Put-Down:* You never stop to think.
*Response:* Yes, I do. Sometimes I just forget to start again.

*Put-Down:* You're so sloppy.
*Response:* It's obvious you don't know my other faults or you wouldn't have mentioned only that one.

*Put-Down:* What's wrong with you that you've never gotten married?
*Response:* Oh, gosh. I knew I forgot something.

*Put-Down:* You don't know what you're talking about.
*Response:* You're not alone in your opinion. My ex-husband felt exactly the same way.

*Put-Down:* You talk too much.
*Response:* I do seem to have a knack for making a short story long, don't I?

*Put-Down:* That outfit makes you look like a clown.
*Response:* Well, that's good, because you sure look like you could use a good laugh.

*Put-Down:* Any put-down meant to personally discount you for belonging to a particular group (short people, overweight people, blondes, etc.).
*Response:* Wait a minute. I *resemble* that remark.

Using humor is a great way to assert yourself and reduce the tension created by a critic's put-downs, inappropriate remarks, or toxic humor. Showing you're not afraid of humor at your own expense is a sure sign of confidence. It preserves your self-respect and enhances you in the eyes of others.

**EXERCISE**

Use the put-downs or negative criticisms you identified on page 129. Think about how you might use the "humor" technique in response to at least two of them.

*EXAMPLE*

> *Put-Down:* An acquaintance approached me at a party saying, "Your earrings certainly call attention to themselves. They're too large and heavy."
>
> *Possible "Humor" Responses:*
>    1. "Too large for what? When it comes to jewelry, my motto is, 'The bigger the better'!"
>    2. Pretending to stagger under their weight, I exclaim, "No, not really!"

## *State Your Position*

One night, when I was out to dinner with some friends, I was commenting how I hadn't shown judgment regarding a decision I had recently taken. My date interrupted, "That's not true, Paulette. You always show judgment...poor judgment!" I knew I had to say something immediately or the unflattering comment would rankle me for the rest of the evening. I turned to him and said kindly, "That's unlike you to be clever at my expense." My date didn't expect to have his motivation for the remark so diplomatically but clearly exposed in front of the others. Chagrined, he apologized. I felt 100 percent vindicated!

Stating your position helps you to stand up for yourself assertively and honestly. It lets people know that they've over-

...ped their bounds and will discourage their inappropriate behavior in the future.

In her book *Say It Right,* Dr. Lillian Glass writes, "If someone is rude—interrupts you, leaves you out of a conversation, is patronizing, or tells an offensive joke—you need to let them know immediately that their comment is unacceptable to you."

The following are phrases you might use to express your position. As you can see, they are simply truthful statements of feelings.

> I don't appreciate your remarks.
> Your comments hurt my feelings. Please don't make them again.
> I disagree with you 100 percent. Saying that was unkind.
> That's an unfair remark. Please don't interrupt me.
> I feel angry at what you said.
> I feel embarrassed by what you said.
> What you said is very disrespectful.
> There's no need for sarcasm.

Stating your position can effectively neutralize or defuse negative comments without the hostility that "fighting fire with fire" usually provokes. As the following example unfortunately shows, too many people don't realize this.

Mitch, aged forty-nine, suffered a knee injury and was no longer able to play his favorite sport, tennis. Zach, his former doubles partner, was enthusiastically discussing his Senior League tennis victory. Mitch interrupted, "How old do you have to be to be in the Seniors, anyway?" Zach, age sixty-five, answered, "Fifty." Mitch laughed derisively and sarcastically said, "Well, then you more than qualify." Zach countered angrily, "Yes, unlike you, Mitch, who will *never* qualify!" Mitch turned on his heel and walked away. The two men never mended their severed friendship.

Mitch's put-down was inappropriate and downright nasty. He was upset and angry at the world because his knee injury knocked him out of tennis permanently. So he lashed out at Zach. Zach's aggressive comeback only increased the animosity between the men. The altercation might very well have been avoided had Zach responded assertively (not aggressively) to Mitch's put-down. Zach could have stated his position by saying, "Please don't take your anger out on me. I understand how angry you must feel about your injury." Of course, Zach could also have used humor to defuse the situation. He could have quipped, "And I get a double membership when I turn one hundred!"

I almost ruined a valued relationship by responding aggressively to an unfair criticism. Fortunately, I saved the friendship with a heartfelt apology and by stating my position.

My friend Nicole forgot to turn her headlights off and woke up to find her car's battery dead. She frantically called and asked me to come with jumper cables to start her car. In my haste, I forgot to make sure that they were in the trunk of my car. I arrived at Nicole's house empty-handed. Nicole verbally attacked me. "Forgetting the cables is really stupid, Paulette. I can't believe you could be so dumb." "You should talk!" I screamed. "Leaving your car headlights on all night isn't exactly intelligent, you know." Nicole shot back, "Go to hell." I knew I needed to demonstrate some verbal fitness immediately if our friendship was to be salvaged. I apologized and stated my position. "I'm so sorry, Nicole. I shouldn't have yelled at you like that. It's just that when you insulted me for forgetting the jumper cables, I wanted to hurt you back. I should have simply said, 'Calling me dumb was very hurtful.'" Nicole apologized also. We hugged each other, laughed in relief, and both ended up being late for work!

As you can see, fighting fire with fire can lead to deep-seated feelings of resentment that will stay with both you and your critic. It will cast an unpleasant shadow on all subsequent dealings you have with that person. Stating your position will more than accomplish your purpose. It will allow you to stand up for yourself and maintain your self-respect by expressing your feelings honestly and openly.

**EXERCISE**

Use the put-downs or negative criticisms you identified on page 129. Think about how you might use the "state your position" technique in response to at least two of them.

*Put-Down:* At a professional meeting, a colleague looked disapprovingly at my outfit and said, "Your skirt is rather short, don't you think?"

*Possible "State Your Position" Response:* "Personally, I think it's just right. That's why I'm wearing it the way it is."

## A Quip for a Quip

At a political dinner, the famous newspaper columnist Ann Landers was introduced to a rather pompous senator. "So you're Ann Landers," he drawled. "Say something funny." Without hesitation, Ann replied, "Well, you're a politician, tell me a lie."

Ann Landers clearly had the gumption and quick wit to trade a "quip for a quip" with the senator. You may find that the other techniques—using humor, genuine inquiry, stating your position, and so forth may not discourage certain critics. Because some individuals are just too arrogant or oblivious to the hurt their verbal digs inflict, giving them a gentle dose of their own medicine may be the only way to penetrate their obtuse thought processes and let them know they've overstepped their bounds. It may be the only way to make a lasting impression on them and let them know you will no longer be the target of their put-down behavior. Remember how well this technique worked for Vicky? When Marc sarcastically referred to her as "Gracie," she playfully referred to him as "George" and suggested he sit in a corner and smoke a cigar! Marc then began treating Vicky with newfound respect.

Another of my favorite trade "a quip for a quip" anecdotes is a historical one involving Winston Churchill and George Bernard Shaw, the famous playwright.

Shaw sent Churchill two tickets to the opening of his new play, with a note: "One for yourself and one or a friend—if you have one." Churchill responded to Shaw's good-natured teasing with a playful retort of his own. He replied that he regretted being unable to attend the opening but asked if it would be possible to have tickets for the second night—"If there is one."

Although few of us are as brilliant and witty as Ann Landers and Churchill, all of us can be successful with this technique. I've compiled a list of comebacks you can use to give verbal bullies a mild taste of their own medicine. I like to call these my "general purpose" quips, as they work well in a variety of situations. Many have been used by comedians, TV interviewers, announcers, and talk show hosts. Some provide a stronger "dose of medicine" than others. Some are quite amusing. Use your favorites whenever you're at a loss for a clever retort to a rude remark.

Be sure to deliver your comeback pleasantly and playfully. Responding in a good-natured way with smiling lips and twinkling eyes will assure your success with this technique. It will help you to come across as assertive rather than aggressive. Read through the list, memorize the lines you like best, and be ready to trade a quip for a quip at a moment's notice. (The last three are from *Funny Comebacks to Rude Remarks,* by Gene Perret, a book you might want to memorize!)

> You remind me of one of Shakespeare's plays—*Much Ado About Nothing!*
> Your mouth costs you nothing. You only open it at other peoples' expense!
> Don't you ever get tired of having yourself around?
> You always speak your mind because you've got nothing to lose.
> Into a closed mouth, no flies will enter!
> You sure know how to pick you friends—to pieces.
> If you don't have something nice to say, keep you mouth closed!
> I'd love to have a battle of wits with you, but it's not fair to fight someone who's unarmed.
> Please give your big mouth a small vacation.
> You're a person of few words—but not few enough.

For those of you who dare to be different, try some of the following quips. All are lifted from works of William Shakespeare and appear in the book *Shakespeare's Insults: Educating Your Wit,* by Wayne Hill and Cynthia Ottchen. Your use of these quotes will probably render your critics speechless with surprise and grudging admiration for your clever assertiveness. They'll think twice before messing with you again!

I profit not by thy talk. *(Troilus and Cressida)*
The empty vessel makes the greatest sound. *(Henry V)*
More of your conversation would infect my brain. *(Coriolanus)*
You speak an infinite deal of nothing. *(The Merchant of Venice)*
What cracker is this same that deafs our ears with this
    abundance of superfluous breath? *(King John)*
Your few bad words are matched with as few good deeds.
    *(Henry V)*
I am weary of your dainty and such picking grievances.
    *(Henry IV, Part 2)*
Beg that thou may'st have leave to hang thyself. *(The Merchant
    of Venice)*

When a bully puts you down, don't get angry—just get up with your
dignity intact. A clever comeback, used in a friendly way, helps you
stand up to any critic. Trading a quip for a quip can do wonders for
your self-esteem. Try this technique with any smartmouth who's
picking on you. You'll feel great about yourself and have some fun
at the same time.

**EXERCISE**

Now that you know a variety of methods for responding to hurtful
remarks and unfair criticism, try this exercise. Show how you might
*agree* with your critic, use *genuine inquiry,* use *humor, state your
position,* or trade a *quip for a quip* in the following ten situations.
Formulate at least three possible responses to each put-down or
snide remark.

*EXAMPLE*

*Situation:* It's quitting time but you're still in your office finishing
up a project. A coworker, on her way home, sticks her head in your
office and says sarcastically, "Working late, huh? I guess you're
trying to score Brownie Points with the boss."

   *Possible Responses:*
   *Humor:* Brownie Points? No way. I'm already a full-fledged
      Girl Scout!
   *Genuine Inquiry:* What are you implying?
   *Agree:* You bet I am!

*State Your Position:* That comment sounded a little snotty. What's the problem?

*Situation:* Your sister is a public defender working for state government. Someone asks her, "When are you going to get a job as a real lawyer?"

*Situation:* After her divorce, a friend moved into a smaller home than she had shared with her husband. Her uncle, feigning concern for her situation, says, "What a shame about your divorce and all. This house isn't as big as the other one and it doesn't have a pool either."

*Situation:* You ask a colleague a question about a company policy you don't understand. She snaps haughtily, "You are so naive. Don't you even know that?"

*Situation:* Your cousin who hasn't seen you in a while drops by. When you tell her nothing is new in her your life, she says, "Don't tell me you're still in that low-paying job!"

*Situation:* You're at a self-service gas station trying to figure out how to operate the pump to fill up your tank. As you're fumbling around, your companion says impatiently, "Oh, come on already. A moron could figure that out."

*Situation:* Your out-of-town in-laws just arrived for a weeklong visit at your house. As your sister-in-law walks in the door, she comments, "I see housekeeping still isn't one of your strong points."

*Situation:* You're chatting with a friend who happens to be overweight. A coworker greets both of you and says to your friend, "That's a great dress. It's amazing how slimming that color is."

*Situation:* You've prepared a lovely meal for several of your husband's business associates and their spouses. Unfortunately, you left the roast in the oven too long and it was slightly overdone. Your husband rolls his eyes and announces to all the guests, "My wife is the worst cook in the world."

*Situation:* A secretary in your office devised a clever plan to streamline a company procedure. A jealous coworker grudgingly congratulates her and then remarks, "Even a blind squirrel finds an acorn once in a while."

*Situation:* After introducing your cousin to several new people, she remarks, "I really like your new friends. They're not dull and boring like all your other ones."

So, how did you do? Were you able to formulate responses using all of the techniques described in the chapter? Don't worry if you drew a few blanks. You can always review the chapter any time and jot down a response as one occurs to you.

This whole business of put-downs and snide remarks is unpleasant, to be sure. It would be great if we didn't have to deal with it, wouldn't it? However, we do. Unfortunately, there's no shortage of social klutzes, or insecure, unhappy people who derive a perverse pleasure from criticizing others or getting a laugh at someone else's expense. Pretending these characters don't exist won't make them go away, but demonstrating the verbal skills you learned in this chapter will yield several positive results.

Some verbal bullies will be discouraged from making you a future target of their jokes or wisecracks. After all, you've become too verbally adept to suit them. They've learned that they can't rattle your emotional cage or give you an inferiority complex. Some bullies and klutzes will actually rethink their behavior, apologize, and change for the better. Some bullies will begin to respect you and may even become your buddies. Most importantly, however, is the result your verbal fitness has on the way you feel about yourself. You will feel empowered with wonderful feelings of courage and confidence. You no longer have to be the victim of unfair criticism, sarcastic remarks, or disrespectful behavior. You no longer have to put up with put-downs unless you want to. Remember, whether you use the genuine inquiry method, agree with the criticism, use humor, state your position, or trade a quip for a quip, *you owe it to yourself to respond!*

# 9

# *Speak Up on the Job*

JoAnn's boss, Brian, is her ever-present shadow. He's constantly looking over her shoulder to see what she's doing or to check her progress on a project, even though she has proven herself to be a highly competent and reliable assistant comptroller. He wants a detailed explanation of how she intends to accomplish a task or solve a problem and then expects a full accounting of how she spends every minute of her time. Frustrated by Brian's management style, and too timid to tell him how she feels, JoAnn is considering looking for another position.

Almost everyone who has ever had a job has experienced feelings of powerlessness or frustration vis-à-vis an employer, supervisor, or colleague. In some places of business, employees are frequently made to feel personally insignificant by employers or coworkers. We all know how emotionally draining this can be. Each of us can tell a story about an indignity we suffered on the job. However, when indignities happen, there are ways to preserve our self-respect and feel good about ourselves.

This chapter presents a variety of ways to help you defuse verbal conflicts, eliminate emotional abuse at work, and just feel good about yourself by communicating assertively on the job.

## The Bully Boss

There are many adjectives used to describe the bully boss: arrogant, tyrannical, intimidating, abusive, and overwhelming, to name a few. Bully bosses may be screamers who verbally attack you in an aggressive, hostile manner. They may disparage you and consider you to be an inferior individual who deserves to be treated contemptuously. Bully bosses have a strong need to be right all the time, and they expect you to comply without question to their mandates. They are quick to display anger or verbal abuse to demonstrate their power over you.

Of course, not all the bullies that you encounter on the job are bosses. They may be coworkers, supervisors, or even clients. There are several ways to assertively deal with these very difficult people.

### GIVE THEM A CHANCE TO LOSE SOME STEAM

Don't allow yourself to be intimidated by the bullies' yelling and bellowing. Look directly at the screamer and wait for her attack to lose some momentum. Once there is a "lull in the storm," you should state your position calmly but assertively.

### STATE YOUR POSITION

It's very important to say something of a standing-up-for-yourself nature to an office bully. As Dr. Robert Bramson writes in his book *Coping With Difficult People*, "The first rule of coping with anyone aggressive or hostile is that you *stand up* to that person. If you let yourself be pushed around by aggressive people, you simply fade into the scenery for them."

Alan Axelrod and Jim Holtje, authors of *201 Ways to Say No Gracefully and Effectively*, suggest taking one of two tacks when confronted with a "screamer." You might say, "Nora, I can't outshout you, and a shouting match wouldn't be very productive anyway. I'm going back to my desk. Let me know when we can have a calm, civil conversation." As an alternative, they suggest using the phrase "hostile work environment." Most employers recognize the phrase and do not want it applied to them, as it has been used in quite a few legal actions taken against employers in cases ranging from sexual harassment to bullying behavior. Axelrod and Holtje suggest saying something to the effect of, "Mr. Stevens, all of this hollering is not only unnecessary and belittling, it is creating a hostile work environment."

Some bullies don't rant and rave. They'll attack you in a well modulated voice with such remarks as, "You are so sloppy, lazy, careless…" or "I can't believe anyone could be so dumb; a moron knows better." Lottie, a nurse, had this type of situation at the medical center where she worked. I recommended she speak up by saying, "Dr. Johnson, you're entitled to criticize my work, and I'll be very pleased to follow your suggestions for improving it. However, you are not entitled to attack me as a person or attempt to make me feel worthless and incompetent." Lottie followed my advice. She later reported that not only did Dr. Johnson stop verbally abusing her, he stopped demeaning the other nurses as well.

Other bully bosses, or senior coworkers for that matter, may habitually take their bad moods or frustration out on you and then later apologize. When they do apologize, don't forgive them. Accepting their apology condones the behavior and gives them permission for another tantrum. Simply deal with these people as you would handle the bullies previously discussed.

### USE ASSERTIVE BODY LANGUAGE

Maintain eye contact with bullies throughout their tirades. This shows in a polite respectful way that you refuse to be intimidated by them. If your bully is standing, you should stand as well. Sitting down while a bully is towering over you does not allow you to project courage and confidence.

### LET BYGONES BE BYGONES

Bullies frequently make friendly overtures to you after you stand up to them. Dr. Bramson analyzes it this way, "This change occurs because the bully, not having been able to overwhelm you, sees you now as worthy of respect." He feels that the bully's change of heart is usually genuine and advises you to "be ready to be friendly." In other words, he cautions you not to hold a grudge. If you are not ready to let bygones be bygones, you will harbor anger and resentment that will get in the way of a productive future relationship.

## Saying "No" on the Job

*Entertainment Weekly* once described how the personal assistants to celebrities in Hollywood are abused. One film producer required his aide to deliver his deposit to a sperm bank. Another demanded that his assistant act as a guinea pig by going on fad diets to see which one worked best. One personal assistant was fired when she refused her boss's 6:30 A.M. command to take his sick son's stool sample to the lab.

Marlee, the director of special events for a large department store chain, was at work the day before she would be leaving on her honeymoon. A movie star had just arrived to promote her new perfume for the chain and wanted "someone of status" in the company's hierarchy to be at her beck and call twenty-four hours a day for the duration of her stay. The company's president told Marlee she was "it." Marlee reminded him that she was going on her honeymoon. Mr. Jonas didn't care and insisted that she be available. Marlee refused his request and was fired.

As I'm sure that you, too, are painfully aware, there are "horror stories" illustrating unreasonable requests made of workers in every profession. Both Marlee and the personal assistant said "no." In order to feel good about themselves and maintain their self-respect, this was necessary. Unfortunately, they were fired. Their employers were dictatorial autocrats who would not accept justified assertiveness. Happily, this is the exception rather than the rule. Most good managers place high value on employee morale. They respect employees and encourage them to express their ideas and feelings.

### "NO, BECAUSE..."

You can frequently minimize the risk to your position or simply avoid feelings of ill will that may arise by offering a valid reason for your unwillingness or inability to comply with a request.

As discussed in chapter 4, "Just Say 'No'," providing an

explanation is not the same as inventing an excuse. Accompanying your "no" response with a brief, honest justification is perfectly acceptable and appropriate.

Analyze the following situations. Consider the possible ways the individual involved could respond to them and the consequences of each choice.

*Situation:* Jocelyn and her husband had an early evening commitment to celebrate their daughter's birthday. Jocelyn's supervisor asked her to work late to finish an important project.

Jocelyn could respond *unassertively* by saying nothing about her plans and staying to work on the project. (This response would cause her to feel unhappy and guilty for disappointing her daughter. Jocelyn would also feel helpless and annoyed with herself for her reluctance to speak up.)

Jocelyn could respond *aggressively* by indignantly exclaiming, "You're always asking me to work late. And your projects are always *so* important. Well, I need to get home to celebrate my daughter's birthday." (Even if such a response didn't cause Jocelyn to be fired, it would probably alienate her employer and cause future friction in their working relationship.)

Jocelyn could respond *assertively* by offering an explanation for her refusal to stay late. She could explain that it's her daughter's birthday and the family has plans to celebrate it together. (Such a response is Jocelyn's most prudent course of action. Any reasonable employer would understand and accept such a refusal.)

*Situation:* Penny's family vacation has been planned for several months based on her boss's previous approval. One week before it will start, Penny's boss asks her to switch her scheduled week off to another time.

Penny could respond *unassertively* by pretending the request is not a problem and change her vacation schedule. (This response would cause her to be upset with herself and her family to be upset, as well. They would all feel cheated because of Penny's submissiveness and inability to speak up.)

Penny could respond *aggressively* by announcing, "You already approved my time off and have some nerve to expect me to change my vacation on such short notice!" (This response is likely to cause Penny's supervisor to become defensive. He or she would probably retaliate by becoming even more adamant that Penny change her plans.)

Penny could respond *assertively* by pleasantly but firmly explaining that she already purchased nonrefundable plane tickets to her destination for herself, spouse, and children. (Such a response would be the most honest, direct way to proceed.)

### "NO. HOWEVER…"

Another good approach to saying "no" is to formulate alternatives whenever possible. A "no" response is much more palatable if you take the time to offer options. Authors Axelrod and Holtje write, "The trouble with no is that it often frustrates the person on the receiving end by making him feel powerless. Counteract this by offering alternatives that empower the person to whom you are saying no: 'While we can't do X, we can do Y or Z.'"

Farah used this technique successfully with a senior vice president in her organization.

At the request of her company's president, Farah coordinated the schedules of the sales reps and vice presidents and arranged a meeting for everyone. Craig, a senior vice president, called a week before and asked her to change the day of the meeting to accommodate his busy schedule. Farah politely refused, "I'm sorry, Craig. I can't change the day of the meeting," and she explained why: "I spent hours coordinating the schedules of two dozen people, all of whom agreed to be there. I can't expect them to change their schedules again." Continuing, she offered, "I'll be happy to meet with you afterwards to give you a full accounting of what transpired. Or, if you like, I'll videotape the meeting for you to view at your convenience." Craig's face lit up, "Great idea, Farah. Have the meeting taped for me."

Farah orchestrated a win-win situation by providing Craig with alternatives. Her self-respect remained high. (She would have felt frustrated and put-upon had she submissively agreed to Craig's unreasonable request.) Additionally, she enhanced herself in Craig's eyes. The vice president now viewed her as a poised, articulate employee who is able to confidently assert herself when appropriate.

Let's see how Jocelyn might have used this approach in her situation. Jocelyn's daughter's birthday celebration precluded her from working late to finish her supervisor's project. Jocelyn had several alternatives. She could have offered to work overtime the following evening; she could have offered to complete the work at home over the weekend; she could have offered to try to find someone else who might be available to work late.

Remember Shirley, the occupational therapist who was unable to refuse patients who asked her to reduce her fees? She felt much better about saying "no" when she had an alternative to offer them. "My fees are not negotiable. However, if you're pressed financially, I'll be happy to work out a convenient payment plan for you" was the perfect response for her.

## TAKE YOUR TIME

Buying time before responding, even when you know you intend to say "no," is another good tactic to use in some situations. It will demonstrate that you honor and respect the request enough to want to think it over. It will also give you an opportunity to formulate a few valid reasons for your "no" and think of some viable alternatives to offer the other party. When it's time to deliver your refusal, be sure to express appreciation, emphasize that your decision was carefully considered, and offer an explanation, alternatives, or both.

Remember Lydia, who hastily accepted a promotion she knew she didn't want because she didn't know how to say "no"? Had she asked for time to think, she would have been ready to decline the offer using the techniques described. The following response would have spared Lydia much personal anguish and aggravation.

"Thank you for thinking so highly of me. Your offer is very

attractive and I gave it careful consideration. I'm not ready to change positions at this point in my career. I can best serve this organization in my present job as head of customer service. If the position is available in a couple of years, I hope you will consider me at that time."

## ASSESS THE RISK

Saying "no" on the job, especially to an employer, is always a challenge. It may involve risk to your professional relationship, further opportunities in the company, or even your position. Only you can determine the degree of risk and decide whether it's worth taking. Offering valid reasons for your refusal to comply with a request and suggesting alternatives is often all that's needed to empower the person to whom you are saying "no" and to win their cooperation. Of course, offering explanations or alternatives may not always be possible, or they may not be acceptable to the other party. Your boss still might tell you some variation of "It's my way or the highway!" So be it. There's no shame in acquiescing if you truly need the job. You expressed yourself and attempted to change an unjust situation. You should be proud of yourself that you made the effort to declare your preference.

## *"Déjà Vu"*

Many of the situations in this section will seem very familiar to you. That's because they probably are! You or someone you know has most likely experienced one or more of them on the job. We've all had to deal with uncooperative or jealous coworkers, bosses that make last-minute requests or look over your shoulder every second, office nuisances, and time-wasters.

## EXERCISE

The following scenarios all require skill and tact to handle constructively. Take some time to decide how you might deal with them confidently and assertively. I've provided sample responses after each situation to give you additional strategies to consider.

*Situation:* Your boss always asks you to do tasks or to find information at the last moment and becomes annoyed when you can't produce results immediately. You usually run around like a "chicken without a head" trying to accommodate her immediately.

> *Don't* become flustered or say, "You are very inefficient to wait until the last minute to tell me what you need. How can you expect me to produce what you want out of thin air?"
>
> *Do* say, "Mrs. Spera, I'd like to be as efficient as possible, *and* I'd like you to look good! I need you to help me do that. Please give me more notice when you need something done. I will do it as quickly as possible and to the best of my ability."

*Situation:* Consider JoAnn and her boss Brian, the ever-present shadow. How would you deal with a supervisor who doesn't give you room to breathe?

> *Don't* say, "I resent your checking up on me constantly" or "Stop looking over my shoulder at what I'm doing every second."
>
> *Do* say, "Brian, I appreciate your interest in my work, but I need you to let me do it independently. I can work faster and more efficiently if you'll ease up on the persistent checking. I'm sure you'll be pleased with my results. And I'll be sure to ask for your advice if I get stuck."
>
> *Do* say, "Brian, when you constantly ask me to account for my time, I feel that you lack confidence in me. I have a proven track record here and always turn in high quality work. Please trust that I will continue to do so.

*Situation:* A coworker is often uncooperative with you. She withholds information you need and gets testy when you ask her for anything that might help you do your job better. You suspect that she's jealous of your success and simply enjoys making your life at the office as difficult as possible.

*Don't* confront her in an exasperated or hostile manner. This
is likely to alienate her further and cause her to retaliate by
becoming even more uncooperative.

*Do* go out of your way to show that you are not a threat to
her. Offer assistance or information that might make her
job easier. Let her know that you appreciate her assistance
or advice and give her credit when she provides it.

*Do* try to make her look good when possible. It's likely that
she'll eventually choose to reciprocate.

*Do* say, "Harriet, I want you to know that you can expect
assistance and cooperation from me; I hope I'll receive the
same from you. Let's have lunch and discuss how we can
both help one another."

*Situation:* A client, colleague, or even your boss habitually wants to
chat pleasantly about insignificant issues unrelated to work. You
don't want to alienate someone trying to be friendly but you've got
work that has to be completed.

*Don't* abruptly say, "Some of us around here have work to do,
so I've got to cut this short," or insincerely say, "Look Ralph,
I'd like to chit-chat (when it's clear you don't), but...."

*Do* politely and specifically explain what you have to do. Say,
"Ralph, I must complete this agenda before the meeting this
afternoon, let's chat later," or "I must return several phone
calls before I leave for the day, please excuse me."

*Situation:* Your supervisor keeps throwing more and more work at
you. It's always, "This just came up," or "I just have one more little
thing for you to do today," or "I volunteered you to help the
comptroller with his survey, I hope you don't mind." You want to be
cooperative but simply don't have the time to do it all.

*Don't* whine, "You give me more work than anyone else.
That's so unfair. Why don't you give some of it to someone
with less to do?"

*Do* explain, "I have a full plate right now. If anything is added
to it, I won't be able to devote the time and attention
necessary to do a good job on everything."

*Do* say, "You know, Joe, there aren't enough hours in the day
for me to complete all these projects this week! I'd like you
to prioritize my work load for me so I can focus on the
most important ones first."

### Handling Put-Downs on the Job

Dr. P. Baron, a surgeon at a major southern university medical
center, chauvinistically believed that female physicians should stick
to pediatrics or gynecology. He enjoyed demeaning his only female
surgical resident, Dr. Sue Ellen Hanes, who was ready to switch her
specialty in order to escape from him and his verbal abuse.

Dr. Hanes, nervously responding to one of Dr. Baron's questions,
began to stammer and trip over her words. In front of twenty male
residents, Dr. Baron announced, as he often did when Dr. Hanes
became flustered, "My, my, Dr. Hanes, I do believe you have a bad
case of 'uterine fibrillation!'" Dr. Hanes had previously asked him
to stop saying that on many occasions. Rationalizing that she had
nothing to lose, as she was on the verge of quitting anyway, she
escalated her response to an unforgettable, "If you ever say that to
me again, *you* are going to have a bad case of 'testicular torsion!'"
(Translation: twisted testicles.) The residents applauded her
display of assertiveness. Dr. Baron merely raised his eyebrows and
never again picked on Dr. Hanes just for the "sport" of it. Dr. Hanes
had finally put an end to Dr. Baron's put-down behavior and
empowered herself by trading a quip for a quip.

In a different situation, Dr. Liz Bloom used the humor technique
to defuse her supervisor's demeaning question. Dr. B. Huston
asked Dr. Bloom a series of technically confusing questions about
hernia surgery. When she was unable to answer any of them, Dr.
Huston challenged, "Do you know *anything at all* about hernias?"
Dr. Bloom's first impulse was to become defensive and respond, "I
know a lot about hernias. It's just that your questions were

misleading." Instead, she feigned a confidence she didn't really feel and joked, "Well, I know I'm glad I don't have one!" Dr. Huston laughed heartily, paternally put his arms around Dr. Bloom's shoulders, and said, "Oh, that's all right my dear, I'll fill you in on what you need to know."

The techniques described in chapter 8, "Don't Put Up With Put-Downs," apply to handling put-down behavior on the job. They usually work whether you are a lawyer, teacher, computer programmer, banker, flight attendant, secretary, or a doctor. In their book *You Don't Have to Take It!*, authors Nicarthy, Gottlieb, and Coffman advise, "If you've been insulted or harassed several times at the same job, you know more or less what to expect. Decide how to answer each type of insult and practice how you might use it in various settings. Ask a partner to give you responses, including interruptions or reactions of other coworkers who might be nearby." They further write that "even if you don't know precisely when you'll be the target of an insult, you can still plan various responses to typical comments. Molly Martin, editor of *Tradeswomen* magazine, says, 'tradeswomen collect comebacks because similar types of harassment and insults occur frequently at certain jobs. It helps to practice. We pass around jokes, comebacks, that we use all the time.'"

Chapter 10, "Go for It!," elaborates on the techniques of anticipating insults, preparing comebacks for them, and practicing these responses in advance of an actual situation.

This next section is designed to give you a bit more practice with typical types of direct and indirect put-down behavior that you are likely to encounter at work.

#### EXERCISE

The following put-down behaviors are regularly experienced by women in workplace situations. Consider which techniques would work the best and how you could respond in each situation. I've provided sample responses after each situation to give you some additional ideas.

*Situation:* You make a suggestion at a department meeting. Your supervisor rolls his eyes in response and asks the others, "Does anyone have anything *worthwhile* to contribute?"

> *Don't* sit by passively looking down at your fingernails while you let her run roughshod over you.
>
> *Don't* defensively mumble, "Gee, I thought what I said was worthwhile. Everyone I discussed it with before the meeting seemed to like it."
>
> *Do* state your position. Look directly at your supervisor. Lean forward in your seat and firmly say, "Pamela, my suggestion has a lot of merit. I discussed it with the floor managers before the meeting and they support it. I'd like to know what part of my suggestion you feel is not worthwhile."

*Situation:* Marty comes up to you while you're eating lunch and publicly berates you for making an error. He talks to you in a scolding manner, as if you were a naughty child.

> *Don't* look away or pretend he's not there.
>
> *Don't* become defensive, make excuses for the error, or profusely apologize for it.
>
> *Do* use the "agree" technique. Stand up to meet Marty's gaze directly. Say, "Yes, Marty, I sent the order to the wrong address. Let's talk about how to solve the problem," or "Yes, I sent the order to the wrong address. I've already contacted UPS to locate it, and I called our client to let him know his order would be delayed a couple of days."

*Situation:* Your boss gives you back a project you've completed saying that it needs to be revised before it can be submitted to corporate headquarters. Before leaving your office, she shakes her head exasperatedly and comments, "Maybe you'll learn to follow instructions some day."

> *Don't* sit there speechless with your mouth dropped open wondering what you did wrong.
>
> *Don't* become defensive, sputtering, "But when I showed you

a preliminary draft two weeks ago, you thought it looked great. You even said I was on the right track."

*Do* request clarification. Say, "Stella, please make your criticism clear. What did you mean just now? Was that meant as a criticism of my work in general? If not, could you be clearer about the specific problems you see with this report?"

In *How to Talk to Anyone, Anytime, Anywhere,* author Larry King says,

> Approach your boss in a completely open manner. Don't appear resentful or fearful of your boss's dissatisfaction. Instead, frame your dilemma like this: 'I have the feeling I could be doing my job more effectively. Could you help me understand what areas I should concentrate on?' or 'I'm not sure I understand how to go about this project. It would help me if you explain what steps I should be taking first.'

*Situation:* One colleague likes to tease you and make jokes at your expense: "It must be nice being the boss's favorite" or "Only the young and cute ones get ahead around here." Another tries to undermine you at every turn, poke holes in whatever you say, and generally squash your ideas: "That'll never work" or "You don't know enough to carry that out." These comments are starting to make you feel insecure and doubt your competence.

*Don't* allow yourself to become rattled or surrender to this behavior.

*Do* state your position. Tell your detractors how you feel about their remarks.

*Do* try to turn your opponents into allies by using the following techniques:

*Ask for their input.* People love to have you value their opinion. Adele Scheele, a career columnist at *Working Women* magazine, advises, "Ask their opinion of something you're thinking of doing, listen to their answer, and then follow up." So, take your next idea to an opponent before proposing it publicly. For example, say, "Desi, I'd appreciate your opinion about something. Can you give me any help or suggestions about how to implement the new performance review procedures?" If you can get a detractor to vest an interest in your idea, it's likely you'll win her support.

*Share the glory.* In her book *Why Good Girls Don't Get Ahead But Gutsy Girls Do,* author Kate White, who has held posts as editor-in-chief at such magazines as *Working Women, McCall's, Child, Mademoiselle, Glamour*, and *Redbook*, writes,

> It's just a fact of life that many of your peers and even some of your subordinates are not going to be overly pleased to see you stepping boldly into the limelight. They may feel jealous, threatened, overwhelmed with a sense that you are on a very fast train and they are being left behind at a dusty little small-town station. They may allow their negative feelings simply to simmer or they may go so far as to act on them, sabotaging what you're doing, criticizing you behind your back. However, if you demonstrate that you are taking them on the train with you by including them in your projects, you have a chance that they will support your efforts rather than hurt them.

### Interrupt Pesky Interrupters

California Senator Bill Lockyer interrupted Assemblywoman Diane Watson while she was speaking to a senate judiciary committee. He told her to stop her "mindless blather." He even added, "I hope I'm offensive enough to make you leave."

Most working women I know lament that male colleagues interrupt them in meetings. I frequently hear, "Every time I try to express an opinion, Harvey cuts me off" or "Whenever I propose a solution to a problem, Jack never lets me finish explaining myself." What do we do about these destructive interrupters? How can we appropriately assert ourselves with these individuals?

Dr. Phyllis Mindell, author of *A Women's Guide to the Language of Success,* recommends asking in private for help from the person who runs the meetings. For example, "When Jack interrupts me all the time, I lose credibility with the others. Could you please ask him to let me finish what I'm saying before you recognize him?" It may also be helpful to personally speak to a notorious interrupter prior to a meeting: "Please don't interrupt me while I'm speaking, Jack. If you don't agree with what I'm saying, let me know afterwards."

Dr. Mindell also suggests building a repertoire of polite ways to say, "Shut up." It's often effective to hold up your hand while saying one of the following:

> Please let me finish.
> I'll be done in a moment.
> I haven't finished yet.
> Kindly hold your questions till I'm done.
> Please hold your comments until the end.

Sometimes individuals will be so oblivious or rude, they will ignore you telling them not to interrupt you. In that event, you'll need to escalate your response to a stronger, *"Please let me finish what I was saying."* That ought to stop the interrupter in his tracks!

I particularly favor the use of humor when appropriate and have found some quips to be effective with certain chronic interrupters. Be sure to deliver them with a twinkle in your eye and a smile on your face. Try:

> I thought I was the speaker and you were the audience!
> John, everyone here would love to interrupt me. I don't think you should have all the fun!
> Excuse me for talking while you're interrupting!
> Would you please give me *five* of the *fifty-five* minutes you used to make a point?

If these don't work, pause for a moment and look directly at the interrupter. Place your hand on his shoulder or arm and say in a well-modulated voice, "I'd really appreciate your cooperation. Please let me finish what I was saying."

Kate White observes that when men attempt to interrupt us women or dismiss our remarks, we respond by sinking into our seat or going the other way, acting shrill, desperate to get a word in.

White cautions women to avoid these responses and advises us to get calmly back into control. She writes,

> One trick I've found helpful for meetings in which a guy is trying to run over your comments is to ask a question of the key person and create an exchange just between the two of you. That gets the ball in your court without making you look desperate. Management consultant Karen Berg says she saw a women reclaim her power in a meeting by standing up and walking around the table as she made her comments. All eyes were totally focused on her.

### Take the Credit

Faye and Lou, law enforcement officers, were asked to develop a presentation that would help improve the police department's image in the community. Although Faye did most of the work, Lou showed the brochures and Power Point presentation to the police chief and took all the credit for her efforts. Faye never said a word and quietly resented Lou's successful effort to receive all the accolades.

Faye considers herself to be an otherwise assertive communicator. After all, she is a respected policewoman who feels comfortable dealing with the public, other law enforcement personnel, attorneys, and even lawbreakers themselves! However, she is typical of many women who are often reluctant to let others know of their accomplishments.

When Faye discussed her situation with me, I suggested that part of being an assertive communicator is not to let other people take credit for her ideas. By remaining silent about this behavior, she simply encourages its repetition.

It's important to nip credit-stealing in the bud! Let the "thief" know how you feel by saying something like, "Both of us were to develop the presentation, yet I had all the ideas and did all the work. I want you to share the work as well as the credit." In the event you decide that your response needs to be escalated with some individuals, try saying, "If you want all the credit, you need to do all the work," or "You know full well the ideas you presented at the meeting yesterday were mine. Next time, 'Give credit where credit is due,'" or even, "Don't let it happen again!"

Author Jean Baer also recommends that if someone takes credit for all your good ideas, put them in writing. Send a memo to your boss with a copy to his or her boss. In her book, *Working Woman's Communications Survival Guide,* Ruth Siress writes, "Women often share their wonderful ideas too openly. Watch out for unscrupulous coworkers who like to pirate ideas and cash in on them. Don't spill your wisdom until you have it documented, dated, and you can prove it's your fine thinking." She also emphasizes that you need to take charge of making yourself look good to your boss, as you can't rely on anyone else to adequately praise you, which brings us to the next bit of advice!

## *Toot Your Own Horn*

A top-level administrator at my college was reading the *Miami Herald* when he noticed an article about the workshops I conduct. He sent me a memo congratulating me, commenting that he never realized the scope of my expertise. I used that as the perfect opportunity to "toot my own horn." I called him on the phone to thank him for acknowledging my work and mentioned that I'd previously received write-ups in the *Washington Post, Chicago Tribune Magazine,* and so on. He asked me to send him copies of those articles, which I did immediately.

As previously mentioned, so many of us are hesitant to let others know of our accomplishments. Innumerable women feel that their accomplishments will speak for themselves and will automatically come to the attention of the right people. Don't count on it! This is not necessarily so. Truly successful individuals know what many others need to learn: "If you don't promote yourself, no one else will do it for you!"

Of course, you don't want to be considered brash or even desperate to hog the limelight. There are several ways to "take the credit" and get noticed for your attainments without being considered a braggart.

## Accept Compliments Gracefully

As discussed in chapter 2, "Adopt Assertive Speech and Body Language," many women are uncomfortable receiving compliments and feel the need to question or qualify them. Hopefully, you are now able to accept a compliment gracefully without diminishing it with self-effacing remarks such as, "Oh, thanks, I was just lucky" or "Thanks, it was no big deal."

Take matters a step further. Use a compliment as an opportunity to talk about your abilities or noteworthy things you've done, as I did when complimented on the *Miami Herald* article. Weave this information into your response to give yourself credit for your attainments.

Wendy used this technique very effectively on the job. Her boss complimented her by saying, "Wendy, you made a fine presentation at the seminar for the new trainees. You're really an asset to the company." She responded, "Thank you. I received excellent evaluations and quite a few memos of appreciation from participants telling me how much they learned. In fact, the presentation was so successful that the director of training and development asked me to repeat it next month for a different group of trainees. Is that okay with you?"

## Use "I" Language

The importance of using "I" language was introduced in chapter 7, "Speak for Yourself." Hopefully, you are now using the pronoun "I" regularly to take credit for your opinions and feelings. It's particularly important to use "I" language on the job to take credit for your accomplishments. Men have no difficulty doing this. Why should we?

In her book, *A Woman's Guide to the Language of Success,* Dr. Phyllis Mindell writes, "Research suggests that women often are so self-effacing that they say things like, 'It's not my achievement; it's their's.' Males, on the other hand, accept the credit for what they've done. The language of success has given you ways to accept credit for your attainments without downplaying or bragging about them."

For example, don't say, "The presentation was a success" or "The company was saved thousands of dollars by implementing the proposed plan" when you could say, "I gave a successful presentation" or "The plan I proposed saved the company thousands of dollars."

Using assertive communication on the job has many advantages. First and foremost, it will enhance your own self-esteem, as Miranda, a research assistant, found out. Here's what Miranda had to say about assertive communication in *You Don't Have to Take It!*: "I gradually became assertive with the boss which both produced good results and left me feeling better. But it didn't always end positively and it was always scary. It did leave me with my self-respect intact."

Using assertive communication will also help you deal with challenging situations and difficult people. You may be pleasantly surprised to find that verbally abusive coworkers and even bully bosses will listen to honest, direct statements of your position.

Using assertive communication will also help you get the recognition you deserve and may even establish the basis for advancement in your career. For example, if you negotiate assertively but pleasantly with your boss on matters of salary and duties, she'll note that you might be well-suited to a leadership position in the company's hierarchy. Speaking up when treated unfairly will demonstrate that your self-esteem is high and you won't let it be undermined. Showing that you respect yourself is likely to gain you the respect and admiration of others. On the other hand, if you're unassertive, you'll be pegged as "wimpy" and won't be seen as "manager material."

Have the confidence that assertive communication works. It may not work all the time, but nothing works all the time! And in the event it doesn't improve a situation, you will still feel empowered for having made the effort. There will be many other opportunities for you to be successful when practicing assertive communication and speaking up on the job.

# 10

# *Go for It!*

While growing up in Queens, my brother and I were the targets of teasing because of our last name, Wainless. The kids in the neighborhood and at school called us "Brainless Wainless." We hated telling our name when we were introduced to new people because we always heard, "Wainless? What kind of a name is Wainless?" or "You mean Wainless, like in Brainless?" These reactions to our name were so common that we learned to expect them!

Our parents suggested that we think of a response that would help us feel better about ourselves and, at the same time, let the wise guys know that they weren't so wise! Together we decided on, "That's really funny, but not very original. We've heard that a million times already." We mentally prepared for the next time we would hear some variation of the "Brainless Wainless" crack. In fact, we could hardly wait for an opportunity to try out our new response. We imagined ourselves feeling confident and secure. We visualized ourselves looking directly into the bully's eyes, holding our heads high, and delivering our well thought out comeback in a clear firm voice. We then visualized the put-down artist looking confused, not knowing what to say next, as we laughed at him! We even enlisted the aid of our parents to help us role-play a typical scenario. Our rehearsal session went something like this:

My Father: What did you say your name is?

Me: Paulette Wainless

My Father: Wainless?

Me: Yes, Wainless.

My Father: How do you spell that?

Me: W-A-I-N-L-E-S-S

My Father: That's a weird name. What kind of name is that anyway?

Me: It's a GREAT name.

My Mother: And what's your name?

My Brother: Ira Wainless

My Mother: Wainless? Like in BRAINLESS? Ha, ha!

My Brother: Ha, ha! That was really funny the first ten or twenty times I heard it.

Our mental preparation, visualization, and role-playing paid off. Our comebacks did the trick. Our critics became deflated by our confident, self-assured attitude. When they realized they couldn't ruffle our feathers with their remarks, they went looking for less verbally fit victims.

### See Things Your Way

Visualization is an extremely powerful technique you can use to gain courage and confidence and become verbally fit. It can help you to achieve specific goals by mentally imagining yourself being successful at whatever you attempt. It helps you to achieve a positive "self-fulfilling prophecy." If you visualize yourself becoming confident and successful, you will probably become confident and successful. If you imagine yourself as popular and well-liked, you'll probably be popular and well-liked. Visualization really works. In his book *Conquer Fear, Overcome Defeat, Abolish Self-Doubt,* Dr. Matthew McKay says:

> Visualization is a powerful, proven technique for refining your self-image and making important changes in your life. Whether or not you believe in its effectiveness doesn't matter.

Your mind is structured in such a way that visualization works no matter what you believe. Skepticism may keep you from trying visualization, but it won't stop the technique from working once you do try it.

Unfortunately, too many people use the technique in a harmful, negative way without realizing it. For example, a student convinces herself that she's going to do poorly on an exam, and she fails it. A hostess convinces herself that her dinner party will be a disaster, and she burns the main course. The graduate convinces himself he's going to make a poor impression during a job interview, and ends up stammering and forgetting what he wanted to say. When I convince myself I'm going to lose my tennis match, I usually double fault on all my serves.

As you can see, we can be our own worst enemies. We sabotage ourselves from being successful at our endeavors by thinking negative thoughts. By the same token, when we think positive thoughts, positive things happen. If the visualization technique is that effective when used negatively, think how effective it can be when used positively!

The night before a recital, a pianist sees herself playing her piece flawlessly. The golfer visualizes that hole-in-one even before picking up his club. Prior to the actual game, a baseball player visualizes himself hitting a home run with the bases loaded. Before going to bed at night, the figure skater mentally sees herself skating perfectly in the Olympics. The tennis star imagines hitting an ace on each and every serve. The actress visualizes the role she's about to play before going onstage. Athletes, actors, musicians, surgeons, and trial lawyers use visualization to prepare for top performances. It works for them. It can work for you, too.

Author Maria Arapakis puts it this way in her book *Softpower!*:

> Your mind is a private rehearsal room where you can try out alternative ways of responding. In the seclusion of your imagination, you can practice dry runs before engaging in the real thing. All it takes is closing your eyes, relaxing, and picturing how a 'best you' would look, sound, and feel. If you can see it in your imagination, you can have it in real life.

A good visualization technique is to imagine how someone else, someone you admire, someone that you feel is extremely poised and articulate, would handle themselves in your situation. Then, you pretend that you're that person. What would *they* say? How would *they* behave if faced with the same situation as you? This technique has worked for me and countless other women on many occasions. First Lady Hillary Clinton, for example, has stated that she likes to imagine how one of her earlier counterparts, Eleanor Roosevelt, would have handled a particular situation. Sometimes, when I'm not sure what I should tell someone, I ask myself, "How would I respond if I were Ann Landers?" Your role model of a charming, assertive communicator doesn't have to be someone famous like Eleanor Roosevelt or Ann Landers! It could be someone you personally know and respect—a friend, teacher, or neighbor. Visualize yourself as an assertive, verbally fit communicator who is respected and admired by others, and you will become an assertive, verbally fit communicator who is respected and admired by others. Think positively and positive things happen. It's as simple as that!

### *Anticipate!*

As discussed in chapter 8, "Don't Put Up With Put-Downs," it's often impossible to know exactly when and where you'll encounter an insulting or hurtful remark. Sometimes these remarks may take you completely by surprise. However, it's often possible to anticipate situations in which you'll need to exercise your verbal fitness skills, and you can prepare for these situations in advance. My brother and I knew from experience that we'd be faced with the "Brainless Wainless" wisecrack time and time again. We decided not to be caught off guard. We brainstormed and came up with assertive comebacks. We visualized ourselves using these comebacks with great success and we role-played anticipated scenarios. Our efforts paid off. We finally felt in control of the situation. More important than that, we felt great about ourselves.

We can all identify situations that cause us discomfort. In fact, just the thought of some of these moments can fill us with dread or anxiety.

For example, Greta dreads her high school reunion every five years. She suffers in silence while Tanya, a former classmate, makes snide remarks about Greta currently "being on her third husband." In a different example, Marisol dreads running into Carlos, a coworker, in the employee lounge. Carlos delights in criticizing her for something petty every opportunity he gets.

Certain situations unnerve us because we believe them to be beyond our control. This lack of control can cause us to feel helpless and anxious, like Greta and Marisol. The techniques of mental preparation, visualization, and role-playing can help us deal with these dreaded situations by teaching us to remain calm and to establish control over our responses.

Both Greta and Marisol could benefit by visualizing a successful outcome to their dreaded situations and mentally rehearsing what they'd like to say. For example, instead of wasting her emotional energy anticipating her feelings of helplessness in the face of Tanya's snide remarks, Greta could come up with a response to Tanya's wisecracks about her "being on her third husband." She would then feel prepared and in control. She could practice such lighthearted quips as, "Yes, Tanya, I'm on my third husband. I finally got it right!" or "Yes, Tanya, I have been married three times. Like they say, 'The third time is the charm!'" Greta could also be prepared with a more potent comeback in the event she wanted to escalate her response to Tanya. "Tanya you're always so obsessed with my husbands! What a shame you have no other topic of conversation. Please excuse me." Having such responses in mind would help Greta project self-confidence and high self-esteem. Just anticipate the situation, visualize yourself coming out on top, and you, too, will find yourself prepared, confident, and in control. You'll no longer need to dread certain situations. Instead, you'll look forward to them and view them as an opportunity to practice your new verbal fitness skills.

Mental preparation also works well when you know you have a stressful situation coming up and want to handle it calmly and efficiently. You might be apprehensive about asking your boss for a raise or for more time off. You might be apprehensive about an upcoming job interview, terminating a relationship, firing an employee, or delivering bad news to someone.

After you've thought about the situation and the words you'd like to say, try writing your thoughts on paper. Once you're satisfied with what you've written, mentally rehearse it. Practice it many times before the actual situation arises, especially when you begin to feel anxious about the upcoming event.

Gwen knew that she intended to tell her husband she wanted a divorce. She mentally prepared and rehearsed for several days before actually telling him. She told me that writing down the gist of what she wanted to say gave her a feeling of confidence and control. Here's what she wrote:

> Herb, I went to see my lawyer last week. I'm filing for divorce. I'm sure this comes as no surprise to you as we've been unhappy together for a long time. I've already made the arrangements and will be moving out tomorrow. My lawyer will be contacting yours. I sincerely hope we can handle this amicably.

Mental preparation also worked for me in a personal situation. When my colleague, Robert, suggested we go out discreetly so his girlfriend Rebecca wouldn't find out, I knew I needed time to mentally prepare a response I wouldn't regret. I spent the evening carefully choosing and mentally rehearsing the words I'd use to decline his invitation. I said them over and over in my mind. "Robert, I adore you. But I have too much self-respect to become involved with anyone who is unwilling to acknowledge me publicly to friends and family. If we still feel the same way about each other when you and Rebecca go your separate ways, we'll revisit this!" I even practiced in front of the bathroom mirror! The next day, I felt confident, secure, and in control of the situation. I was able to deliver my message matter-of-factly and assertively.

**EXERCISE**

Create your own personal hierarchy of situations in which you are generally reluctant to speak up or take action. Order them from 1 to 10 to indicate in which situations you find it more difficult to assert yourself. (The higher the number, the more difficult it is for you to be assertive in that situation.) Some of the following situations may be personally relevant to you. You might like to consider them when creating your hierarchy:

- complaining to a physician for treating you rudely or abruptly
- speaking up about receiving a lesser product or service than you expected
- asking for your deposit back on a product or service you no longer want to buy
- sending back improperly prepared food in a restaurant
- calling attention to an overcharge on a bill
- declining an invitation to a social event or for a date
- saying "no" to unwanted houseguests
- asking a friend to return money she borrowed
- speaking up if someone cuts in front of you in line
- returning a defective product to a store
- speaking up to a colleague who refers to you by some "pet name" you don't like
- saying "no" to a friend's request to borrow a favorite possession

Now get a sheet of paper and write down your list of ten situations in order of difficulty. Analyze your responses. Describe how you could use mental preparation and visualization to rehearse what you'd really like to say when actually faced with the situation. Begin with the situations you find to be the least threatening and progress to those in which you experience the most difficulty speaking up.

*Example:* Two weeks ago, your friend Sally borrowed $20, promising to return it the next day. You would like it back.

> I close my eyes and picture myself meeting Sally for a pleasant informal lunch, something we both do often. I picture myself reminding her that she owes me $20 and ask her when she'll return it. I imagine the actual words I'd like to use. "Sally, by the way, I wanted to remind you about the $20 I loaned you two weeks ago. I'm sure you've just forgotten about it. When can I expect you to pay me back?" Again, I picture Sally in my mind. I pretend she's sitting across the table from me. I

visualize her friendly apology and offer to pay me back. Now I practice the words aloud. I hear myself say, "Sally, by the way, I wanted to remind you about the $20 I loaned you two weeks ago. I'm sure you've just forgotten about it. When can I expect you to pay me back?" I repeat the words several times to become comfortable with them.

## EXERCISE

This next exercise is slightly different. It includes situations in which many women would find it particularly difficult to speak up. Read each situation and circle the number on a scale of 1 to 5 that best indicates how easy or difficult it would be for you to communicate assertively in that situation. (1 represents *easy;* 5 represents *difficult*)

*Situation:* A coworker is extremely offensive to work with. While he doesn't direct his remarks to you personally, he frequently uses foul language and makes vulgar remarks about others. You'd like to tell him to stop this behavior.      1 2 3 4 5

*Situation:* Your boss often berates you in front of others for making minor mistakes. She recently lashed out at you for temporarily misplacing the key to the supply cabinet. You want to tell her to stop criticizing you in such a demeaning way.      1 2 3 4 5

*Situation:* You suspect your housekeeper of stealing from you. Several items of sentimental value have disappeared from your house over the last few months. You want to find out what your house-keeper knows about this.      1 2 3 4 5

*Situation:* You and your friend are shown to a small table for two in a restaurant. You'd prefer to sit at a larger table. Several are available. When you ask to switch, you're told the larger tables are for parties of three or more. You really want to change tables.      1 2 3 4 5

*Situation:* Your supervisor often takes out his bad      1  2  3  4  5
moods on you and then later apologizes. You are
tired of being his punching bag. You want to tell
him that apologizing does not exempt him from
exercising self-control.

*Situation:* Identify your own situation that generally    1  2  3  4  5
causes you to feel stressed or unnerved.


Now, analyze your responses. As with the previous exercise, begin
with the situations you find to be the least threatening. Get a sheet
of paper and a pen and write down how you might mentally
prepare yourself and rehearse your responses using visualization.

There is another good strategy you can use to remain calm and
prepare yourself for any anxiety producing situation. It utilizes the
techniques of mental preparation and visualization already discussed. Basically, it involves anticipating all the details associated
with what you want to say and imagining them happening just as
you'd like them to. Experiencing the scenario several times in your
imagination helps you to feel confident and in control when you
actually face the situation in real life. It's important to visualize the
situation with as many details as possible. Where are you? What
time is it? Who else is in the room? What are the other people in the
room doing? Be sure to break the situation down into specific
steps. Work your way through them in chronological order.
Imagine them occurring one by one. Psychologists recommend
that you even write your steps down.

For example, Lonnie's boss puts a note on her desk saying he'd
like to see her first thing in the morning. Lonnie suspects that he
wants her to be in charge of local arrangements for the company's
national sales convention for the fourth year in a row. This involves
negotiating with hotels, arranging accommodations and transpor-
tation for out-of-towners, contracting with caterers for the annual
banquet, organizing entertainment—in short, a major time commitment. Lonnie dreads telling him that she doesn't want to do it
again. Yet, she's determined to stick to her guns, and decline the
assignment. Lonnie visualizes the situation exactly as she expects it

to unfold. She imagines herself handling herself assertively and remaining steadfast in her position. Here's what Lonnie wrote:

1. I arrive at the office half an hour early to give myself time to relax and have a cup of coffee before meeting with Mr. Stevens.

2. At 8:55 A.M., I walk over to Mr. Stevens's office.

3. I smile and say "Good morning" to his secretary, Delia.

4. I ask Delia, "Do you have any idea what Mr. Stevens wants to see me about?"

5. Delia replies, "I'm not sure, but I think he wants you to chair the local arrangements committee again.'"

6. Deila opens the door to Mr. Steven's office and announces me.

7. Mr. Stevens invites me to sit down and have a cup of coffee, which I accept.

8. I say, "I got your note yesterday, Mr. Stevens. How may I help you?"

9. Mr. Stevens clears his throat and asks me to chair the local arrangements committee.

10. I take a deep breath, look directly at Mr. Stevens, and pause before speaking.

11. I calmly and confidently let him know that I prefer not to chair the committee again this year.

12. Mr. Stevens protests as I expected he would, and attempts to make me feel guilty by telling me that he was counting on my experience and expertise.

13. Still looking directly at him, I remain steadfast in my assertion and repeat my position.

14. Mr. Stevens sighs and asks if I'll at least show the ropes to whomever he finds to chair the committee.

15. Responding, "Of course, that would be my pleasure," I stand up, shake his hand, and leave his office.

Lonnie read over her list several times before her actual meeting with Mr. Stevens. She felt confident enough to handle the situation even if it didn't play out exactly the way she imagined it would. A situation that she once thought would be difficult turned out to be a piece of cake.

Of course, there's always the possibility that the situation won't play out as smoothly as you'd like. After all, you have no control over the other person's reaction. You only have control over your own. It may be helpful to imagine the worst case scenario and how you would successfully handle that as well.

### EXERCISE

Use a situation you identified in the previous exercise or one you actually have coming up that causes you to feel apprehensive. Do what Lonnie did. Break it down into specific events that you can visualize.

You may also find it helpful to use a systematic step-by-step strategy that utilizes mental preparation and visualization. I adapted the following approach from an exercise in defusing, which author Mary Lynne Heldmann describes in her book *When Words Hurt: How to Keep Criticism From Undermining Your Self-Esteem.*

*Step 1* involves making a list of the various verbal bullies and critics in your life. Write down who they are and what they tend to criticize you about. Do their put-downs or negative comments have a consistent theme? Do they always criticize you about the same thing (for example, your weight, social life, choice of friends, domestic abilities, a particular personality trait, etc.)?

*Step 2* involves mentally preparing and formulating responses to each unfair criticism or put-down. Write them down so you can refer to them whenever you like. Read your responses aloud several times to become comfortable with them.

*Step 3* involves visualization. Visualize a situation in which one of your verbal abusers or bullies is picking on you. See and hear yourself confidently delivering your possible responses. Heldmann even suggests that you really have some fun with this exercise by picturing your critic in his or her underwear. I enjoy visualizing my critics in as many unflattering ways as possible, for example, in their underwear or even naked, with no hair, with no teeth, with warts all over their face. This always makes me smile and relax whenever I feel anxious about standing up to toxic people in my life. Heldmann writes,

> Visualize the exchange between you and your critic, using the defusing responses you have just written. Hear the words that your critic says. Then hear yourself defusing each criticism. Feel yourself staying calm and in control. Hear yourself speaking steadily and confidently. Enjoy the sense of achievement that is rightfully yours after you have defused the criticism. Be sure to smile and feel the joy of success. This sends a strong positive message to your subconscious.

**EXERCISE**

Take a clean sheet of paper. Use the three-step approach just described and make your list. Be sure to complete all three steps for each critic you identify.

*EXAMPLE*

*Step 1:* I feel like Linette looks down on me for being a stay-at-home mom. She makes me feel insignificant because I chose to be a housewife rather than work outside the home.

*Step 2:* "You know Linette, we all make choices in life. I respect your choice to have a career. Please respect my choice to stay at home and raise my family."

*Step 3:* I imagine running into Linette waiting in line at the bank. I visualize her harried and unkempt, with stains on her dress, scuffs on her shoes, and runs in her stockings. I hear her ask me in a loud, unflattering voice, "Still at home all day doing nothing but watching soap operas?" I hear myself confidently use the "agree" technique and reply, "Yes, I'm still at home all day. I escaped for a few minutes to take care of some banking business." Then I hear her say, "Seriously, how can you stand staying home all day doing nothing." I visualize myself smiling pleasantly and responding,

"You know Linette, we all make choices in life. I respect your choice to have a career. Please respect my choice to stay at home and raise my family." I then visualize all the observers to this exchange looking at me with respect and admiration for the way I handled myself. I feel great because I didn't allow Linette's toxic comments to bother me as they usually do.

### *When in Doubt, Act It Out*

Role-playing is yet another great technique to help you rehearse and be prepared for real-life situations. It enables you to practice and experiment in anxiety-free settings so that you become comfortable and confident enough to handle high anxiety situations when they arise. All you'll need is a little imagination and a friend or relative to help you.

Jean Baer, author of *How to Be an Assertive (Not Agressive) Woman in Life, Love, and on the Job,* provides an excellent set of guidelines for using role-playing in your program of practice for real life. I've outlined some of the key ones as follows:

1.  Focus on one specific situation to role-play at a time. Don't deal with more than one problem during any specific practice session. If your boss unfairly criticizes you in front of others, frequently expects you to work late, and asks you to run errands which are not in your job description, choose just one of the problems for your role-playing session. For example, stating your position when she publicly puts you down for minor oversights.

2.  Enlist the aid of a friend or relative to be your role-playing partner. Be sure to choose someone with whom you feel comfortable and uninhibited.

3.  Explain the situation and personality characteristics of the other party to your partner. Give your partner specific directions about playing the role of the other party. Role-play the situation. When you're finished, analyze how it played out. Discuss with your partner what you liked about your performance and what you'd like to improve.

4. Role-play the situation again. This time, try it with the changes you and your partner discussed.

5. Now role-play the situation again with the roles reversed. Have your partner model what you should say while you imitate how you expect the other party to act in the real-life situation. Discuss the results with your partner.

Jean Baer advises that you not get discouraged if the role-playing doesn't work completely or solve your problems. After all is said and done, you might still not get what you want. You might not "reform" the verbal bully or change the way your boss behaves toward you. You might not get an unfair bill reduced or a refund to which you're entitled. However, you will feel empowered because you practiced assertive communication and made a wonderful effort to stand up for yourself.

It's often helpful to role-play the situation with your partner pretending to be as difficult and uncooperative as possible. This will prepare you for the "worst that could happen" and help you get through that as well. You will probably find that the worst case scenario isn't really all that bad!

Remember how the thrice-married Greta dreaded seeing Tanya at their high school reunion? Here's how Greta might role-play to prepare for neutralizing the sarcastic comments that she expects Tanya to make at the upcoming event:

1. Greta asks her mother to role-play the anticipated scenario with her.

2. Greta explains to her mother that Tanya likes to goad her because of her multiple marriages. She encourages her mother to be as "sarcastic" as possible in her role as Tanya. Their role-playing session might go something like this:

Mother: Hello, Greta. It's so nice to see you again.
Greta:  Hello, Tanya, It's nice to see you, too.
Mother: So, how many more times have you been married since we've seen each other last?

> Greta: Oh, at least seventeen. I'm not sure. I've lost count!
>
> Mother: Seriously now, Greta. You're still with your *third* husband?
>
> Greta: Yes, I'm still with my third husband. Isn't it great I finally got it right?
>
> Mother: Don't you think three times is a bit excessive?
>
> Greta: Like they say, "The third time is the charm." It was so nice speaking to you, Tanya. I see someone over there I'd like to say hello to. Enjoy the party. (Greta confidently walks away with her head held high.)

If Greta wanted to escalate her response in the event Tanya still didn't shut up, she could be much more direct, as in the following response:

> Greta: Tanya, you're so obsessed with my husbands. That's all you ever talk about. I'm starting to think that you're ready for a change. Call me if you want some marital advice. See you around.

Remember my student Diane, who received an unfair bill from a roofing company? Before she called the company back to protest the charges, I encouraged her to formulate a "That's not acceptable" response using the six-step approach outlined in chapter 6. Since she was nervous about dealing with the abrasive Mrs. Manning, I suggested we role-play the scenario together first. This helped reduce her anxiety and gave her confidence so that she would not become intimidated by the Mannings under any circumstances. I played the role of both Mrs. and Mr. Manning. Here's how our rehearsal session played out:

> Me: Hello. Manning Roofing, may I help you?
>
> Diane: Hello Mrs. Manning. This is Diane Smith. I'm calling to ask you to reconsider adjusting my bill.
>
> Me: I already told you that I wouldn't do that. You owe us $450.
>
> Diane: Mrs. Manning, your refusal to reduce my bill is not acceptable.

Me: Really? How did you figure that?

Diane: The roofer didn't have to replace any tiles. Less work was done than described in the original estimate.

Me: Look. We gave you an honest estimate. You accepted it. You owe us the full amount of $450.

Diane: As I stated, the roof repair was less involved than originally thought. Mr. Manning included the cost of replacing roof tiles in his original estimate. This turned out not to be necessary. It's unethical to ask me to pay for work that wasn't done.

Me: Why are you wasting my time with this? You owe us $450.

Diane: I want you to adjust my bill and charge me only for the actual work done.

Me: I can't do that.

Diane: I'd like to speak to Mr. Manning please.

Me: He's busy right now. He can't come to the phone.

Diane: When will he be available?

Me: Later this afternoon.

Diane: Thank you. I'll call back around 4:00 P.M.

Me: It won't do you any good.

Diane: Hello, Mr. Manning. I'm sure your wife told you how I feel about your bill and why it should be reduced.

Me: Yes, young lady, she did. But I agree with my wife. You owe us $450.

Diane: Your roofer did a nice job. I'd like to recommend your company to others.

Me: We hope you do. But we still can't reduce your bill.

Diane: Mr. Manning, I'm sorry it has come to this. I will not send you anything until my lawyer advises me what to do. Furthermore, I intend to call the Better Business Bureau.

You'll recall, the upshot was that Mr. Manning finally agreed to reduce Diane's bill to $350!

**EXERCISE**

Choose three of the "That's not acceptable" situations described in chapter 6. Write out a script showing how you might role-play these situations with a partner. Better yet, find a partner to actually role-play these scenarios with you!

The techniques of mental preparation, visualization, and role-playing can help you to become verbally fit and greatly increase your confidence. They can get you warmed up and in condition to say what you feel. When you're actually ready to speak your mind, you'll be ready and at ease. The situation won't seem so threatening or new. You'll be comfortable and confident as you'll feel like you've faced it many times before—even if only in your mind!

### *Confident Communication Is a Lifetime Skill*

Assertive, confident communication has many rewards. It will help you get what you want and need more often. It will help you say "no" when you want to. It will help you say "yes" with conditions and to state your conditions. It will enable you to say "I don't know" or "maybe" and to ask for time until you decide what you want to do. It will empower you to take responsibility and credit for your own words and actions. Assertive communication will help you express yourself freely and confidently. It will help you to be a positive role model for your children and increase their chances of developing into verbally fit, confident adults.

As with trying out any new skill, you may feel unsure of yourself at first. Remember the first time you ever rode a bicycle? And now? I'm sure you mount your bicycle easily and confidently. Well, with practice, the ability to communicate assertively will also become second nature to you. It will help you gain courage and confidence. So, go for it. You've got nothing to lose and everything to gain!

# *Appendix:*
# *Raising Assertive Children*

Ruth came from a background where her family never expressed their thoughts and feelings or spoke up for themselves. She and her sister learned from *their* unassertive parents, who had learned from their unassertive parents. Ruth doesn't want her children to turn out the same way. She doesn't want them to grow up as she did—too timid to complain about unfair or disrespectful treatment, or allowing others to take advantage of her good nature. Ruth wants to be a better role model for her children than her parents were for her.

Psychologists report that assertive parents produce assertive children. By watching you communicate assertively with others, your children will develop the ability to communicate assertively themselves. They will be able to stand up for themselves, be self-confident, and have self-respect. If you communicate openly and directly with others, your children will learn to communicate in the same way.

Avoid demonstrating insecure, passive, or timid behavior. If your daughter hears you say, "I've never been good with numbers," she'll probably decide she can't be good in math. If she sees you silently accepting poor service or disrespectful behavior, she'll decide she doesn't deserve better treatment either. If you constantly inconvenience yourself or always sacrifice your needs for others, she'll allow herself to be used. She'll put herself last, and she'll feel she is only worthwhile when serving others. Let your daughter see that you can appropriately express and share your feelings. Let her also see that you're sure of your rights and that you know how to stand up for them.

So, read this book with your children, especially your daughters. Young women endure the most distress from timidity and passivity. They will greatly profit by adopting an assertive communication style. Help them as youngsters. You can do this by providing opportunities for them to speak for themselves in a variety of situations.

*Allow your children to answer questions meant for them:* "What's your name, Sweetie Pie?" the pleasant saleswoman asks your daughter. "Her name is Susie," you say. "How old are you now?" the woman continues. "She just turned three," you tell her, beaming. This scenario sounds familiar, doesn't it? Many mothers are guilty of answering questions directed to their children. Resist the urge to answer for them. Allow your children to speak for themselves.

Conversely, there are times when someone directs a question to you as if your child weren't present. "What's her name?" "How old is she?" Invite that individual to inquire directly of your child. Try saying, "Susie is right here. Please ask her." Make every effort to include children in conversations, especially conversations about them. Let them see you value their participation in the discussion and what they have to contribute to it.

*Encourage your children to resolve problems independently:* "Mom," my eight-year-old son whined, "I lost my quarter in the video game machine. Please tell someone." "No, Jeremy," I said, "You tell someone. Find the manager. Be sure to ask for a refund." Jeremy returned triumphantly five minutes later with another game machine token.

"Aunt Paulette?" "Yes, Sweetheart?" I responded to my four-year-old niece. "My hot dog is cold in the middle. It doesn't taste good," she replied handing me her food. Sure enough, it was not fully cooked. I said, "Stephanie, I'll call the waitress. When she comes, I'd like you to bring the problem to her attention. Ask her to please bring you one fully cooked." Stephanie did just that!

"Mommy look," lamented Nicole. "My new backpack is tearing at the ~~~~~~~~~~~~ Will you exchange it while I'm at school?" "No," said her mother, "I'd like you to accompany me so you can explain the problem yourself." Nicole confidently strode over to the customer service counter declaring, "I just got this backpack and it's defective. Please exchange it for another one." Nicole was given a new one immediately.

Resist the urge to come to the rescue and fix your children's problems. Involve them in the problem-solving process. As child psychologist, John Rosemond, Ph.D., writes in *A Family of Value,* "The more parents do for a child, the less the child is ultimately capable of doing for himself. Granted, parenthood requires that we run a bit of interference. Parents must be ready to buffer, deflect, and even eliminate certain kinds of problems. But the facts are these. You cannot run constant interference for a child and then expect that as an adult he will successfully anticipate and deal with life's problems." This applies perfectly to the challenge of developing assertive communication in our children. The more parents speak for their children and solve their problems, the less likely the children will develop the confidence to speak for themselves later in life.

My now thirteen-year-old son used to be concerned that the person "in charge" wouldn't pay attention to him because he was "just a kid." I assured him that I would come to his rescue and "run interference" if necessary. Feeling more secure that he had a safety net if he needed one, Jeremy became willing to take the first shot at solving his own problems. More often than not, there was no need for me to intervene. So before you take care of the difficulty, encourage your children to speak for themselves. Jeremy and Nicole, for example, now have the confidence to make the effort to resolve their own problems. I'm sure you'll be pleasantly surprised that the same will hold true for your children.

*Allow your children to make inquiries and verbalize their own requests:* "Mom, I have to go to the bathroom," Jeremy announced in a large department store. "Where is it?" "I have no idea, Jeremy. I suggest you inquire and find out."

Again, resist the urge to make inquiries on behalf of your

children. Give them the opportunity to speak for themselves. If your daughter needs to use the restroom in an unfamiliar place, have her find out where it is. If you can't find her favorite cookies at the supermarket, have her ask where they are. If you don't know where an item is at the toy store, teach your daughter to ask, "Can you please tell me where to find the computer games?"

While eating out, encourage your children to order for themselves. If your son wants a well-done, plain hamburger, let him place the order. If your daughter wants a vanilla sugar cone with chocolate sprinkles, let her request it.

At the pediatrician's office, allow your children to tell the doctor what's wrong and describe how they feel. You can always fill in any important details later.

*Encourage your children to ask questions when they don't understand something:* At Mesa Verde National Park in Colorado, a park ranger was conducting a guided tour of a 1,500-year-old native American Indian cliff dwelling. She invited the group to ask questions after her lecture. I overheard an eleven-year-old whisper to his mother, "What does Anastasi mean?" "Mitchell," the woman told her son, "I really don't know. Please ask the ranger for both of us." Mitchell beamed as the ranger provided an interesting explanation and praised him for his great question.

*Reinforce your children for demonstrating independence and expressing opinions, and observations:* When my son's friends tried to convince him to take karate lessons with them, he said, "I don't like karate. I'd rather take tennis lessons after school, even if I don't know anyone else in the class." I told him, "I'm really proud of you for sticking to your guns by not allowing your friends to influence your decision." If you observe your child telling a playmate she is unhappy with the friend's behavior, say, "I'm really pleased you told your friend she was rude to ignore you at the party."

Prompted by her father, I observed a rather precocious little girl tell the manager of a movie theater that the ladies' restrooms were dirty and should be cleaned. The harried manager thought he was being funny by remarking, "When I want your opinion, I'll give it to you." The child countered, "I'm perfectly capable of expressing my own opinions, thank you. We'll just go to the movies somewhere else next time!" Her father complimented her, "That was a great comment, Loren. I'm really glad you said what you did. I agree with you one hundred percent!"

*Encourage your children to show gratitude and pay compliments:* Be a good role model in this area. If your children observe you showing approval and gratitude, they will learn to do so as well. Make comments like, "I really like that outfit you put on this morning," "You did a great job on your math homework," "Thank you so much for helping me carry the groceries from the car," or "That was a terrific idea. You were absolutely right!" Parenting expert Sandra Hardin Gookin, author of *Parenting for Dummies,* advocates writing notes to your kids as one way to praise them for a job well done. She suggests a note in their lunch box: "You did a great job making your bed this morning! Thank you so much. We love you, Mom and Dad."

Christine read that her daughter's classmate Brian won a prize at the county youth fair. She urged her daughter to call and congratulate him. Christine heard her daughter say, "Congratulations, Brian. My mom just told me about your prize. We're very happy for you."

Billy mentioned his friend Naomi passed her scuba diving certification test. His dad urged him to call her. "Way to go Naomi. That's great news about getting your scuba certification," he praised.

Jared's older sister was all dressed up for her high school prom. Jared's dad prompted him to tell her how nice she looked. He was pleased to hear Jared compliment her. "You look really cool Tiffany. You look great in that dress."

Beginning with his first airplane trip when he was two years old, I'd always prompt Jeremy to thank the pilot and flight attendants as they said goodbye to the disembarking passengers. Jeremy now does so spontaneously. He generally shows his appreciation by saying, "Thanks for a great flight."

*Encourage your children to offer condolences and apologies when appropriate:* Encouraging your children to offer apologies and express condolences goes a long way toward helping them develop assertive communication skills. Alice's friend's dog, Sparky, died. Her mother encouraged her to offer her condolences. Unsure of what to say, Alice asked her mother for some ideas. How about something like, "I'm so sorry to hear about Sparky. I know how sad you must feel. Please remember I'm your friend. Call me if you feel like talking," her mother suggested.

Connie asked her five-year-old son if he remembered to say thank you to the "cookie lady" at the supermarket. He had forgotten. Connie accompanied him back to the bakery section so he could apologize for his forgetfulness. In a tiny high pitched voice he said, "I'm sorry I forgot to say thank you for the cookie." The kindly woman behind the counter replied, "That's okay, Honey. We all forget important things once in a while. Here's another cookie for remembering!"

*Encourage your children to share their thoughts and feelings:* Let your children know that you are interested in what they have to say. Using such expressions as "Tell me more about it," "Keep going, you're doing great," or "I'm always interested in what you have to say" shows you consider your children's feelings important. It's important to use appropriate body language at the same time. For example, encouraging your children to share feelings while you read the newspaper or watch TV will negate your best intentions. You will give the impression you don't really care, that your television show or newspaper article takes precedence over their concerns. Sit at the same level and maintain eye contact with your children while they are speaking to you. Keeping your words and body language in sync with them will show your children that you really are interested in them and that what they're saying is important to you. Don't feel you always have to arrive at a solution to your child's problem or fix what's wrong if your child is upset. Simply act as a sounding board. Lend a sympathetic ear to encourage your children to express their feelings.

Allowing your children to speak for themselves teaches them to take credit and responsibility for their actions, needs, and thoughts. When children speak for themselves, it builds their self-confidence because it gives them control over life's situations. It is necessary for them to learn to function independently. Teaching your children to make their own requests, praise others, solve their own problems, express their own opinions without fear of ridicule, and share their feelings will increase their confidence that they are competent individuals who can succeed in life. They will effortlessly develop into assertive and positive individuals.

# Bibliography

Alberti, Robert E., Ph.D., and Michael L. Emmons, Ph.D. *Stand Up, Speak Out, Talk Back!* New York: Pocket Books, 1975.

_____. *Your Perfect Right.* 7th ed. San Luis Obispo, Calif.: Impact Publishers, 1995.

Alderman, Ellen, and Caroline Kennedy. *The Right to Privacy.* Westminster, Mass.: Knopf, 1995.

Arapakis, Maria. *Softpower! How to Speak Up, Set Limits, and Say No Without Losing Your Lover, Your Job, or Your Friends.* New York: Warner Books, Inc., 1990.

Axelrod, Alan, and Jim Holtje. *201 Ways to Say No Gracefully and Effectively.* New York: McGraw Hill, 1997.

Baer, Jean. *How to Be an Assertive (Not Aggressive) Woman in Life, in Love, and on the Job.* New York: The Penguin Group, 1976.

Bower, Sharon Anthony, and Gordon H. Bower. *Asserting Your Self.* Reading, Pa.: Addison-Wesley Publishing Co., 1994.

Bramson, Robert M., Ph.D. *Coping With Difficult People.* New York: Dell Publishing, 1988.

Brumfield, Shannon, Ph.D. *Fix It Before It Breaks.* Byron, Calif.: Front Row Experience, 1995.

Canfield, Jack, and Mark Victor Hansen. *The Aladdin Factor.* New York: Berkley Books, 1995.

Capozzi, John M. *If You Want the Rainbow, You Gotta Put Up With the Rain.* Fairfield, Conn.: J M C Industries, Inc., 1997.

Carter, Jay. *Nasty People.* Chicago: Contemporary Books, 1989.

De Angelis, Barbara, Ph.D. *Real Moments.* New York: Dell Publishing, 1995.

Ellis, Albert, Ph.D. *How to Stubbornly Refuse to Make Yourself Miserable About Anything.* Secaucus, N.J.: Carol Publishing Group, 1988.

Glass, Lillian, Ph.D. *Say It Right.* New York: Perigee Books, 1992.

_____. *Toxic People.* New York: St. Martin's Griffin, 1997.

Gookin, Sandra Hardin. *Parenting for Dummies.* Foster City, Calif.: IDG Books Worldwide, Inc., 1995.

Heldmann, Mary Lynne. *When Words Hurt.* New York: Ballantine Books, 1990.

Hill, Wayne, and Cynthia Ottchen. *Shakespeare's Insults: Educating Your Wit.* New York: Random House, 1995.

Horn, Sam. *Tongue Fu!* New York: St. Martin's Griffin, 1997.

Jeffers, Susan, Ph.D. *Feel the Fear and Do It Anyway.* New York: Fawcett Columbine, 1988.

King, Larry. *How to Talk to Anyone, Anytime, Anywhere.* New York: Random House, 1994.

McCall, Timothy B., M.D. *Examining Your Doctor.* Secaucus, N.J.: Carol Publishing Group, 1995.

Mindell, Phyllis, Ed.D. *A Woman's Guide to the Language of Success.* Englewood Cliffs, N.J.: Prentice Hall, 1995.

Nicarthy, Ginny, et al. *You Don't Have to Take It!* Seattle: Seal Press, 1993.

Nierenberg, Juliet, and Irene S. Ross. *Women and the Art of Negotiating.* New York: Barnes and Nobel Books, 1997.

Perret, Gene. *Funny Comebacks to Rude Remarks.* New York: Sterling Publishing Co., Inc., 1990.

Rosemond, John, Ph.D. *A Family of Value.* Kansas City: Andrews and McMeel, 1995.

Sanford, Linda Tschirhart, and Mary Ellen Donovan. *Women and Self-Esteem.* New York: Penguin Books, 1985.

Sarnoff, Dorothy. *Never Be Nervous Again.* New York: Ivy Books, 1987.

Siress, Ruth Herrman. *Working Woman's Communications Survival Guide.* Englewood Cliffs, N.J.: Prentice Hall, 1994.

Spera, Stephanie, Ph.D, and Sandra Lanto, Ph.D. *Beat Stress With Strength.* New York: DBM Publishing, 1995.

Swink, Linda D. *Speak With Power and Grace.* Secaucus, N.J.: Carol Publishing Group, 1997.

Tannen, Deborah, Ph.D. *That's Not What I Meant.* New York: Ballantine Books, 1987.

―――――. *You Just Don't Understand.* New York: Ballantine Books, 1991.

Van Ekeren, Glenn. *Speaker's Sourcebook II.* Englewood Cliffs, N.J.: Prentice Hall, 1994.

Walters, Lily. *What to Say When You're Dying on the Platform.* New York: McGraw-Hill, Inc., 1995.

White, Kate. *Why Good Girls Don't Get Ahead but Gutsy Girls Do.* New York: Warner Books, 1996.

# Acknowledgments

*"Be Wealthy in Your Friends"*

—WILLIAM SHAKESPEARE

Regarding my friends, even Shakespeare would agree that I am a millionaire several times over. I may be the mother of my book but it was conceived and delivered with the help of many!

My love and gratitude to:

Ellen Karsh, who first urged me to write a book and along with Barbara Burt, Tommie Ems, Dr. J. Terence Kelly, and Kathleen Watson, who read the manuscript, offered valuable insights, and sharpened my thinking on all issues.

Dr. Shannon Brumfield and Diane Gabriel Sloan for their keen observations; Eileen Lemberger for her enthusiasm and typing the manuscript; Alberto Meza for his great illustrations.

Patricia Smith and Michael Snell, fabulous literary agents, for guiding me through the proposal process; Carrie Cantor, my editor with Birch Lane Press, for her astute suggestions and fine-tuning of the manuscript.

Melody Chaykin, Blanca Ortega, Cathy Rosenfeld, Shirley Pearson, Angel Mohammed, Dr. Paul Perito, Mahlia Perito, Wendy Schmidt, Martha Bentancur, J. B. Veltman, and my many students and workshop participants who brainstormed ideas and generously shared their stories and anecdotes with me.

And finally to my son, nephew, and niece. Jeremy Maxwell Dale, Daniel Max Wainless, and Stephanie Anne Wainless, who are already en route to becoming confident, assertive, and happy adults who will experience life as a blessing, not a burden.